Legal Identity, Race and Belonging in the Dominican Republic

T0352579

Legal Identity, Race and Belonging in the Dominican Republic

From Citizen to Foreigner

Eve Hayes de Kalaf

ANTHEM PRESS

Anthem Press
An imprint of Wimbledon Publishing Company
www.anthempress.com

This edition first published in UK and USA 2023
by ANTHEM PRESS
75–76 Blackfriars Road, London SE1 8HA, UK
or PO Box 9779, London SW19 7ZG, UK
and
244 Madison Ave #116, New York, NY 10016, USA

First published in the UK and USA by Anthem Press in 2022

Copyright © Eve Hayes de Kalaf 2023

The author asserts the moral right to be identified as the author of this work.

British Library Cataloguing-in-Publication Data
A catalogue record for this book is available from the British Library.

Library of Congress Control Number: 2023930570

ISBN-13: 978-1-83998-829-5 (Pbk)
ISBN-10: 1-83998-829-0 (Pbk)

The cover photo was taken by Lorena Espinoza Peña featuring the
Dominican anthropologist Juan Rodríguez Acosta.

This title is also available as an e-book.

In loving memory of my friend, colleague and mentor
Phillip Wearne, who, whenever I wanted to give up, always replied:
'Kenbe fèm, pa lage!'[1]

---

1. Hang in there, keep going (Haitian *kreyòl*).

CONTENTS

FIGURES

FOREWORD

Junot Díaz

It's been ten years since the Dominican Republic issued its infamous Sentencia, a malevolent ruling that it retroactively stripped hundreds of thousands of Dominicans of their citizenship, plunging many more into a condition of permanent legal precarity. On the back of this single decision, the country stomped on its constitution, its international obligations and nearly a century of jus soli citizenship in order to target the black collectives that right-wing Dominican elites had long sought to undermine.

As an artist who has made the Dominican Republic his life's work, I have long believed that my island is the ground zero of the New World – which is to say that much of the armature of what we call modernity was first beta tested on Ayiti and Quisqueya. Whether we're talking about the Plantationocene or coloniality or our toxic racial politics or our endless resistance to all of these, the island is, for better or worse, a crucible from which our global futures are first glimpsed before they spread occultly over the rest of the world.

It was clear from jump – to me and many others – that the Sentencia would, if not resisted, be the future of us all.

Much could be said about the tumultuous months of that struggle: the countless trips to Santo Domingo, the collaborations and the solidarities; the klaxon we sounded to alert the larger world; the disinformation and hate campaigns the government spread to gag and vilify its critics; the troll armies it unleashed; the accusations of treason directed against all who raised their voices in protest; the torrent of online threats against the so-called traitors; the fear and silence these tactics produced. But what stays with me still, and continues to inspire, is the courage of those who refused to back down in spite of all the threats and opprobrium. The incredible bravery of those who could not avail themselves of the protections and privileges that activists like me enjoyed in the States.

One thing is for certain: in the midst of that madness, that whirlwind – when some of us were filing with the United Nations, and others were speaking out in forums and organising marches and trying to raise funds and awareness – there was the sense, in my circle at least, that the Sentencia was far deeper and more complex than we could immediately grasp, with roots that far exceeded the Dominican context, but which we could not coherently trace at that time.

If only then we had had Eve Hayes de Kalaf's eye-opening book at our disposal. How enrichened our understanding would have been. How much that was obscured would have been dragged into the light.

If you're going to read one account of the Sentencia, then Legal Identity, Race and Belonging in the Dominican Republic: From Citizen to Foreigner is the one. Hayes de Kalaf tells the entire terrible tale of the ruling – from its earliest intimations in the racialised dictatorship of Rafael Trujillo to the peculiar political conjuncture that finally made this old dream of the Dominican ultranationalist into a reality, to its impact, both on the island and abroad. Hayes de Kalaf brings to her account the meticulous depth of a scholar and all the zealous truth-seeking of a journalist, untangling all the complex forces that went into this devil's brew. She lays bare the political horse-trading that would transform former president Leonel Fernández, the poster child of the new progressive technocratic Dominican Republic, into the button man for the island's most reactionary political factions.

If this book were a straight-ahead chronicle of what led up to the nightmare it would be invaluable, deserving of its place of pride on every human rights shelf. But Hayes de Kalaf goes further; imbedding the Sentencia within a global context to reveal how the international push for birth registration as a solution to the global problem of under-documentation helped provide the anti-immigrant, anti-Black, anti-Haitian, anti-poor elements in the Dominican Republic with an opportunity and rationale to disenfranchise whole sectors of the Dominican people.

Even more significantly, Hayes de Kalaf takes time to centre those people directly impacted by the Sentencia – their quest to secure the 'proper' documentation, to negotiate the racist and arbitrary barriers arrayed against them and to understand how one day they could be Dominican and the next day find they are not. In a series of oral history interviews that are sometimes wrenching, sometimes infuriating and always eye-opening, Hayes de Kalaf seems to take on the entire breadth of the Dominican nation – Dominicans of Haitian descent, Anglo-descended 'cocolo' Dominicans, Japanese-Dominicans, even a white Dominicana born of Argentinian parents.

What we learn in this process is there is not one Sentencia, but many, and what is the end of the world for one is but a frustrating annoyance for another. If it is true that the consequence of our dire politics lives most fully in its victims, what is also true is that not everyone chooses to see themselves as a victim, and that variability matters profoundly if we hope to relate to the human element within our political abstractions.

In the end this is not a book, in Toni Morrison's famous turn of a phrase, to pass over. This book is vital. The silences it breaks are deep and entrenched and dangerous. Only ten years have passed since the Sentencia was unleashed, and yet, already much has been forgotten or distorted, and despite the amount of uproar the Sentencia caused at the time it is not all that easy to find good solid information on this supreme violation of human rights. Even as I write these words, deportations in Dominican Republic are increasing and the wave of anti-immigrant politics is, once again, on the rise across our world.

No: this is not a book to pass over.

PREFACE

This book offers some uncomfortable insights into the use and abuse of modern-day identity-based development 'solutions' for exclusionary and citizenship-stripping practices. It is the culmination of a long personal, intellectual and transformative journey that began in the Dominican Republic and has taken me around the world. Born from a desire and dedication to amplify the lived experiences of everyday Dominicans, this book includes the often overlooked, ignored or forgotten voices in contemporary debates about statelessness, citizenship, legal and, increasingly, digital identity.

This book is a cautionary tale regarding the rapid expansion of global identification measures which aim to provide universal legal identity in the run-up to the 2030 UN Sustainable Development Goals (SDGs). This study is the first to link the promulgation of contemporary ID practices by international organisations, such as the World Bank, the United Nations (UN) and the Inter-American Development Bank (IADB), with practices implemented by the state to arbitrarily and retroactively strip citizenship from Dominican-born Black citizens of (largely) Haitian ancestry.

I show that while identification programmes, and the digital technologies that support them, strive to include marginalised groups, they also have the potential to exclude some 'users' from these systems. I use policy analysis, archival research and oral history interviews[1] to illustrate how citizens have been forced to navigate complex bureaucratic systems and overcome seemingly unsurmountable hurdles, in order to retain or gain access to their Dominican legal identity.

The island of Hispaniola is shared between the Dominican Republic (to the east) and Haiti (to the west). For over eighty years, the Dominican Constitution recognised the right of 'all people born on Dominican territory' to *jus soli*

---

1. The interviews for this book were carried out as part of my doctoral studies at the University of Aberdeen. I summarise the findings of this research in the chapter: E. L. Hayes de Kalaf, 'Making Foreign: Legal Identity, Social Policy and the Contours of Belonging in the Contemporary Dominican Republic', in *Welfare and Social Protection in Contemporary Latin America*, ed. G. Cruz-Martínez (London: Routledge, 2019).

(birthright) citizenship.[2] For decades, however, nationalist politicians and some lawmakers ignored this constitutional guarantee and instead vehemently rejected the claims of Haitian-descended people to Dominican citizenship.[3] This included persons who not only already identified as Dominican citizens but also had the paperwork to prove it.

As we will see in this book, tens of thousands of persons of Haitian ancestry found themselves in a fierce battle to (re)obtain their legal identity when the authorities began to reject their requests for paperwork on the grounds that their parents were born 'in transit' or 'residing illegally'.[4] Disputes over who the state should recognise as Dominicans culminated on 23 September 2013 in the now notorious Constitutional Tribunal decision 168-13 (the *Sentencia*).[5] The *Sentencia* centred on Juliana Deguis Pierre, a documented woman of Haitian ancestry. Civil registry officials were refusing to renew her birth certificate, which she needed to acquire a national identity card. *Sentencia* judges decided that the irregular migratory status of Deguis Pierre's parents at the time of her birth exempted their daughter from Dominican citizenship. As a result, they determined she had retrospectively inherited the 'illegal' status of her parents and subsequently invalidated her birth documentation. Deguis Pierre, they decided, was not, nor could she ever have been, a Dominican citizen. She was rendered stateless by this decision.

In an attempt to diffuse tensions, and in response to strong international indignation to the ruling, the former Dominican president Leonel Antonio Fernández Reyna claimed the *Sentencia* was necessary as it would help rectify anomalies within the civil registry, some dating back over eighty years. He lamented that, in his opinion, there were still people living in the country who, like Deguis Pierre, had wrongly received their legal identity documentation, thus leading them to assume that they were Dominican citizens. He stated:

---

2. Children born to 'diplomats' and persons 'in transit' were the two exceptions to this rule.
3. For key arguments that reject the automatic right of persons of Haitian ancestry to birthright Dominican citizenship, see J. M. Castillo Pantaleón, *La nacionalidad dominicana* (Santo Domingo: Editora Nacional, 2012).
4. N. Sears, 'Repealing Birthright Citizenship: How the Dominican Republic's Recent Court Decision Reflects an International Trend', *Law and Business Review of the Americas* 20 (2014): 423–48 (426). See also International Human Rights Clinic, 'Justice Derailed: The Uncertain Fate of Haitian Migrants and Dominicans of Haitian Descent in the Dominican Republic', Report of the International Human Rights Clinic, Johns Hopkins School of Advanced International Studies, 2015.
5. *Sentencia* TC/0168/13, *Referencia: Expediente número TC-05-2012-0077*. Santo Domingo, 2013.

If [the *Sentencia*] is retroactive then there has been a problem determining the legal status of people living in the country. They have been under the impression they are Dominican and, at some point, were even in possession of [Dominican] paperwork. Something like that can lead to other types of problems.[6]

I was in a unique and privileged position to carry out the research for this book. I am a dual British-Dominican national having naturalised as a Dominican citizen after several years living and working in the Caribbean. Thanks to my national identity card (*cédula de identidad y electoral*), I had voted in the national elections, owned a credit card, held a local driver's licence and travelled on my Dominican passport. When news of the *Sentencia* broke in 2013, I found it inconceivable that I – a white, foreign-born European woman – would continue to benefit from my status as a Dominican when hundreds of thousands of Black Dominicans born in the country abruptly found themselves stripped of their nationality.[7] The sense of injustice at the decision was palpable and the main motivation for me writing this book.

During the time I lived on the island, I had seen just how overwhelmingly cumbersome and seemingly Kafkaesque registrations could be. Many Dominicans call the civil registry *el tollo*, which literally translates as *atolladero*, meaning 'mess'. For many, their interactions with the civil registry were often painstakingly bureaucratic and frustrating. I had experienced first-hand how my foreign birthplace, race and social status placed me in a position of privilege above Black Dominicans, Haitian migrants and Haitian-descended groups. Disgracefully, I was regularly allowed to skip queues at government offices and given priority over others, many of whom had to wait for several hours to be seen by a state official.

A number of years ago, I attempted to cross the Dominican-Haitian border on a public bus. Immigration officials stopped me, stating they were suspicious as to why I was travelling on a Dominican passport. I was detained, taken to a back office and interrogated as to whether I was a *dominicana neta* (a *real* Dominican). It was only years later that I came to realise I was not stopped and questioned solely because the documents I was carrying aroused suspicion. My interaction with the border officials depended on a variety of 'social factors, including the situation in which they were presented, the audience

---

6. Hayes de Kalaf, 'Making Foreign', 102: 'Si tiene un efecto retroactivo [...] entonces implicaría un problema determinar el estatus legal de quienes han vivido en el país, que han tenido la impresión de ser dominicanos y en algún momento tuvieron hasta la documentación dominicana, y eso engendra otro tipo de problemas'.
7. I talk about Dominican nationality and citizenship interchangeably in this book.

witnessing the event, a calculation of [my] social capital, and judgments made about [my] class, status, and race' (Bartlett et al., 2011). My experience was intrinsically linked not only to how my papers identified me but also to how I was perceived in my interactions with others.

In stark contrast to my experience at the border, each time I flew from the Dominican capital Santo Domingo to the Haitian capital Port-au-Prince, I was able to travel with relative ease. Not once was I challenged over the authenticity of my identity documentation or my status as a Dominican. At this moment, because of my social capital, the documentation I was carrying and the expectations the border officials had regarding my behaviour and appearance, I was not stopped or questioned. I concluded it was expected that I would choose to travel by plane rather than spend many hours on an uncomfortable bus journey. I was interrogated at the border precisely because I looked out of place. It was not only the documents I had on my person that aroused suspicion, but the fact that, to the border guards, I did not belong in that space as a white woman holding a Dominican document. Although my ID card and passport proved that I was a citizen, to the border guards who questioned me, I would, beyond question, always be a foreigner.

Using the Dominican Republic and the lived experiences of persons of (largely) Haitian ancestry as a case study, this book illustrates the contestations that have arisen over access to a legal identity, including the practical problems documented citizens have faced in proving to the authorities that they are Dominicans. I underline how, particularly for migrant-descended people of African heritage, legal identity practices have exacerbated disputes over who should be granted access to identity documentation and who ultimately states decide to include as citizens. This book therefore offers a timely critique of global policy measures which over the next decade are striving to allocate all persons, everywhere, with their own legal identity.

ACKNOWLEDGEMENTS

I am indebted to so many people who have encouraged and helped me complete this book over the past six years. Notably, my PhD supervisors Trevor Stack and Nadia Kiwan at the Centre for Citizenship, Civil Society and Rule of Law (CISRUL), University of Aberdeen and Karen Salt (University of Nottingham) as well as Linda Newson and Ainhoa Montoya at the Centre for Latin American and Caribbean Studies (CLACS), University of London. I would also like to thank my former lecturers and staff at the Institute of the Americas, University College London (UCL): Kate Quinn, Graham Woodgate, Maxine Molyneux and Par Engstrom. I want to acknowledge the support I have received from friends and colleagues at the Haiti Support Group past and present: Christian Wisskirchen, Andy Leak, Mario Gousse, Shodona Kettle, Kasia Mika, Antony Stewart, Paul Sutton, Rachel Douglas, Anne McConnell, Leah Gordon, Charlotte Hammond and Angela Sherwood. This study would not have taken place without the phenomenal support I received from Phillip Wearne, my late colleague, friend and comrade whose passion for social justice and informed activism has created an irreplaceable vacuum and to whom I dedicate this book.

The scholars, writers and activists who have assisted me in developing this project include the phenomenal Junot Díaz, who needs no introduction. I would also like to thank Ernesto Sagás (Colorado State University), David Howard and Diego Sánchez-Ancochea (University of Oxford), Samuel Martínez (University of Connecticut), Jørgen Sørlie Yri (Norwegian University of Science and Technology), Leiv Marsteintredet (University of Bergen), Gibrán Cruz-Martínez (Spanish National Research Council), Ana María Belique Delba (Reconoci.do), Bridget Wooding of the Caribbean Migrants Observatory (OBMICA), Kristy Belton (International Studies Association), Laura van Waas, Amal de Chickera and Natalie Brinham of the Institute on Statelessness and Inclusion (ISI), Laura Bingham (Open Society Justice Initiative), Nicholas De Genova (University of Houston), Chuck Sturtevant (Davidson College) and Alison Phipps and Giovanna Fassetta (GRAMNet, University of Glasgow). A big thank you also to Katherine Tonkiss (Aston

University) and Marieke Riethof and Charles Forsdick (University of Liverpool) for helpful edits, comments and suggestions.

To the fantastic Frank Báez and Giselle Rodríguez for their years of friendship, kindness and encouragement, and for facilitating access to the private collection of the late sociologist Francisco Bienvenido Báez Evertsz and the library at the Fundación Global Democracia y Desarrollo (FUNGLODE). To Altair Rodríguez, José Horacio Rodríguez and Miguel Ceara-Hatton for their intellectualism. To Lorena Espinoza Peña for her tireless activism and photo for the front cover of this book which features the Dominican anthropologist Juan Rodríguez Acosta. I am especially grateful to Kiran Jayaram (University of South Florida), April Mayes (Pomona College), Karen E. Richmann (Kellogg Institute for International Studies/University of Notre Dame), Elizabeth Manley (Xavier University of Louisiana) and everyone else at Transnational Hispaniola for welcoming me into their flock as a budding Dominican scholar. Thanks also to the wonderful and talented scholars who attended the conference Global Dominican – Politics, Economics and Cultural Production at Senate House, University of London, in 2018. This includes the organisers Conrad James (University of Birmingham), Catherine Davies and William Tantam of the Institute of Latin American Studies (ILAS), University of London, and Maria Thomas (Goldsmiths), as well as the participants Lauren (Robin) Derby (University of California), Maria Fumagalli (University of Essex), Lorgia García-Peña (Harvard University), Kimberly Simmons (University of South Carolina), Silvio Torres-Saillant (Syracuse University), Raj Chetty (St John's University) and Fernanda Bustamante (Autonomous University of Barcelona).

Last but not least, I would like to thank my beautiful daughter, Leila, and my friends, family and loved ones in the Dominican Republic. *Sin la paciencia y el apoyo de ustedes, este trabajo nunca hubiese sido posible. Por eso estoy eternamente agradecida.*

ABBREVIATIONS

ADESS	Administradora de Subsidios Sociales (Social Grants Administration Department, Dominican Republic)
CARICOM	Caribbean community
CCTs	conditional cash transfers
CDD-PIPS	Componente Dotación de Documentos Legales de Identidad, Proyecto de Inversión en la Protección Social (Legal Identity Documentation Component, Social Protection Investment Project, Dominican Republic)
CEDESO	Centro de Desarrollo Sostenible (Centre for Sustainable Development, Dominican Republic)
CERSS	La Comisión Ejecutiva Para La Reforma del Sector Salud (The Executive Commission for Health Sector Reform)
CRC	Convention on the Rights of the Child
CRC4D	Civil Registration Centre for Development (CRC4D)
DNRC	Dirección Nacional de Registro Civil (National Directorate for Civil Registrations, Dominican Republic)
EFEC	Escuela Nacional de Formación Electoral y del Estado Civil (National School for Electoral and Civil Status Training, Dominican Republic)
END	Estrategia Nacional de Desarrollo 2030 (National Strategy for Development 2030, Dominican Republic)
FNP	Fuerza Nacional Progresista (National Progressive Force, Dominican political party)
FTZs	free trade zones
FUNGLODE	Fundación Global Democracia y Desarrollo (Global Foundation for Democracy and Development)
GCPS	Gabinete de Coordinación de las Políticas Sociales (Technical Directorate of the Social Cabinet, Dominican Republic)

IACHR   Inter-American Court of Human Rights
            (Corte Interamericana de Derechos Humanos)
IADB   Inter-American Development Bank
            (Banco Interamericano del Desarrollo)
ICCPR   International Covenant on Civil and Political Rights
IMF   International Monetary Fund
            (Fondo Monetario Internacional)
IOM   International Organization for Migration
ISI   Institute on Statelessness and Inclusion
JCE   Junta Central Electoral
            (Central Electoral Board, Dominican Republic)
MEPyD   Ministerio de Economía, Desarrollo y Planificación
            (Ministry for Economy, Development and Planning,
            Dominican Republic)
MIP   Ministerio de Interior y Policía
            (Interior Ministry and the Police, Dominican Republic)
MOSCTHA   Movimiento Sociocultural para los Trabajadores Haitianos
            (The Sociocultural Movement of Haitian Workers, Dominican
            Republic)
MUDHA   Movimiento de Mujeres Dominico-Haitianas
            (Movement of Dominican-Haitian Women, Dominican
            Republic)
NGO   non-governmental organisation
OAS   Organization of American States
OBMICA   Observatorio Migrantes del Caribe
            (Caribbean Migrants Observatory, Dominican Republic)
OSJI   Open Society Justice Initiative
PIPS   Proyecto de Inversión en la Protección Social
            (Social Protection Investment Project, Dominican Republic)
PLD   Partido de la Liberación Dominicana
            (Dominican Liberation Party)
PNRE   Plan Nacional de Regularización de Extranjeros en Situación
            Migratoria Irregular en la República Dominicana
            (National Regularisation Plan for Foreigners in an Irregular
            Migratory Situation in the Dominican Republic)
PRD   Partido Revolucionario Dominicano
            (Dominican Revolutionary Party)
PROSOLI   Progresando con Solidaridad
            (Progressing with Solidarity, Dominican Republic)
PRSC   Social Christian Reformist Party
PS   Programa Solidaridad

	(Solidaridad Programme, Dominican Republic)
SCJ	Suprema Corte de Justicia
	(Supreme Court of Justice, Dominican Republic)
SCRAL	Social Crisis Response Adjustment Loan
SDGs	Sustainable Development Goals
SEE	Secretaría de Estado de Educación
	(Secretary of State for Education, Dominican Republic)
SIUBEN	Sistema Único de Beneficiarios
	(Unified Beneficiary Identification System, Dominican Republic)
UDHR	Universal Declaration of Human Rights
UIS	Unidad de Información Social
	(Unit of Social Information, Dominican Republic)
UN	United Nations
UNHCR	The UN Refugee Agency
UNICEF	United Nations Children's Fund
UNDP	United Nations Development Program
WCAR	World Conference against Racism, Racial Discrimination, Xenophobia and Related Intolerance

Chapter 1

ID: AN UNDERAPPRECIATED REVOLUTION

'Con papeles no se come', pero ellos pueden ayudar a comer mejor.
['We can't eat our papers', but having paperwork will help us eat better.].[1]

Today, an estimated one billion people around the world have no formal proof of identity, and many citizens continue to lack even the most basic form of documentation. Supported by the international development sector and met with enthusiasm from global tech companies, data controllers and industry specialists alike, the en masse registration of populations has exploded in recent years. Already a multimillion-dollar industry, the improved targeting and identification of individuals around the world is now a game changer on the international stage. Laurence Chandy, director of Data, Research and Policy at the United Nations Children's Fund (UNICEF), recently called the prioritisation of documentation within global policy, including the transition from paper to digital identity systems, 'one of the most under-appreciated revolutions in international development'.[2]

This chapter examines contemporary efforts to provide universal legal identity in accordance with the UN Sustainable Development Goals (SDGs).

---

1. A. Pichardo Muñiz, *Proyecto de Inversión en la Protección Social (PIPS) Estudio Línea Base y Evaluación del Impacto* (Santo Domingo: Gabinete de Coordinación de Políticas Sociales, 2014), 8 (all translations of the interviews from Spanish to English and Haitian kreyòl to English are author's own).
2. 'The evolution of identification programs from birth registration to national ID cards to digital IDs. Since the year 2000, over 130 countries have started digital ID programs – surely one of the most under-appreciated revolutions in international development.' This original comment was made on Twitter by Laurence Chandy, the director of Global Insight and Policy at UNICEF, 2018, https://twitter.com/laurencechandy/status/953453745416953856.

The SDGs aim to 'provide [a] legal identity for all' by 2030.[3] This means that over the coming decade, states around the world will prioritise the implementation of registrations to ensure that every person on the planet obtains their own birth certificate. We will learn how important the concept has become for international development planning as it is widely assumed to foment the inclusion of all citizens and is therefore seen as a necessary tool in the fight against informality, under-documentation and statelessness.[4]

Legal Identity and the Sustainable Development Goals: A Warning

In alignment with the expansion of neoliberal reforms, since the 1990s identity systems have grown to become a central pillar of the global world development agenda. Formal identification is now considered a 'prerequisite for development in the modern world' (Gelb and Clark, 2013) and policymakers have actively promoted the implementation of pro-poor policies that encourage the improved targeting, identification and documentation of domestic populations to ensure they can access any welfare payments or aid assistance to which they are entitled. International organisations have supported the expansion of identity measures that target the income-poor and the marginalised with particular zeal, often assuming systems that register and document individuals to be largely inclusionary.[5] They have contributed high levels of financial and technical assistance to governments to improve civil registries as a means to ensure that all citizens can access their paperwork.[6]

---

3. United Nations, *Transforming Our World: The 2030 Agenda for Sustainable Development*, Goal 16 (New York: United Nations, 2015), 28: 'Promote peaceful and inclusive societies for sustainable development, provide access to justice for all and build effective, accountable and inclusive institutions at all levels.' Goal 16.9: 'By 2030, provide legal identity for all, including birth registration'.
4. For this book, the term 'undocumented' refers to a person never recorded within a civil registry with no documentary evidence of citizenship. I apply the term 'informal' to populations that may possess some form of paperwork but do not yet hold all their legal identity documents such as a birth certificate and identity card together with a unique identifier number.
5. World Bank, *Inclusion Matters: The Foundation of Shared Prosperity* (Washington, DC: World Bank Group, 2013).
6. Campaigns that actively promote legal identity include the Global Campaign for Equal Nationality Rights, the UNHCR's #IBelong Campaign to End Statelessness by 2024 and its Global Action Plan to End Statelessness: 2014–2024, the World Bank's 'ID4D' platform, the 2014 Brazil Declaration and Plan of Action, the Africa Programme on Accelerated Improvement of Civil Registration and Vital Statistics, and the Regional Strategic Plan for the Improvement of Civil Registration and Vital Statistics in Asia and

The provision of legal identity hinges on the institutional capacity of states to determine the effective identification of their citizens through the issuance of documentation. This system depends intrinsically on the goodwill and cooperation of states to recognise, record and document their own nationals. It rests on the understanding that citizens must possess official documentation to facilitate social inclusion, access to welfare and further rights.

In September 2015, the UN General Assembly adopted legal identity as a core and cross-cutting aim of the SDGs. The successful implementation of this goal rests on the principle that a legal identity guarantees the protection of rights for the individual.[7] Despite becoming central to all development planning, a comprehensive explanation of the term is still being debated in policy circles and no formal definition exists within international law (Manby, 2020, p. 250). The Inter-American Development Bank (IADB), for example, defines legal identity as

> a composite condition obtained through birth or civil registration which gives the person an identity (name and nationality) and variables of unique person identifiers, such as biometrics combined with a unique legal number.[8]

The World Bank links the concept to

> identity (a rights- and status-based concept), registration (a system for recognizing and recording rights and status), and documentation (an instrument of proof).[9]

Legal identity, therefore, is not just about the recognition of status; it demands evidentiary proof of status.[10] For the purposes of this book, I interpret

---

the Pacific. The World Bank, the IADB, the Asian Development Bank, the International Organization for Migration, the UN Refugee Agency and the United Nations Children's Fund have all actively promoted the universal registration of citizens.

7. This definition was shared with me by Mia Harbitz, former employee of the IADB during a Skype interview on 16 July 2019.

8. IADB, 'Democratic Governance, Citizenship, and Legal Identity: Linking Theoretical Discussion and Operational Reality', IADB Working Paper, 2009, 4.

9. The World Bank Legal Review, *Financing and Implementing the Post-2015 Development Agenda: The Role of Law and Justice Systems. Volume 7* (Washington, DC: International Bank for Reconstruction and Development/World Bank, 2016), 106.

10. As the Open Society Justice Initiative argues, 'proof of legal identity is fundamental for ensuring that all people are able to access their rights, including the right to acquire nationality, essential services, and other identity documents'. See OSJI, *A Community-Based Practitioner's Guide. Documenting Citizenship & Other Forms of Legal Identity* (New York: Open Society Justice Initiative, 2018), 7.

legal identity as the formal recognition of a person's name and nationality before the law through the provision of state-issued documentation such as a birth certificate, a national identity card or a passport.[11] I acknowledge that legal identity can be linked to other forms of ID, such as a driving licence, but principally I am concerned with how it can be used to tie an individual to their national status and access to services. Our legal existence, then, does not simply depend on our recognition as citizens within law; increasingly, it also depends on our ability to prove that we belong to a state.

While policymakers, international development specialists and practitioners overwhelmingly see identity-based development policies as inclusionary, the 'administrative ordering' (Scott, 1998, p. 4) of populations through the use of large-scale identification practices has led to atrocious human rights abuses (Seltzer and Anderson, 2001). This is particularly true for individuals who, due to their race or national origin, do not always fit comfortably within state-centred, ideological and white-centric notions of who merits membership of the 'imagined community' (Anderson, 1983). Supported by a well-managed bureaucracy, the (re)ordering of the German civil registry in the 1930s led to the identification and elimination of the 'administrative existence' (Torpey, 2000, p. 166) of Jews under Nazism. National identity cards were central to the identification and murder of the Tutsis during the Rwandan genocide (Fussell, 2001). In the United States, states would strategically deny state membership to the native-born, including women, Indigenous, Black and foreign-descended populations. This form of 'citizenship by design' (Zolberg, 2006) tailored policies along Eurocentric ideals of 'whiteness', reserving citizenship for an elite minority.

In recent years, the introduction of digital ID systems and practices in the borderlands of western Myanmar has subjected the Rohingya to a process of 'bureaucratic cleansing' (Brinham, 2019, p. 157) following nationwide crackdowns on political dissent. In Kenya, officials have used biometric systems to record Somalis as foreigners (Weitzberg, 2017) despite their belonging to the country's 'Indigenous' population. In 2010, the British Home Office took the decision to destroy the landing cards that evidenced the legal and settled status of the Windrush generation (Tonkiss, 2018). Trapped in a catch-22 situation, Black Britons were asked to produce a document that no longer existed to evidence they had entered the United Kingdom lawfully. Some lost their

---

11. At the Hague Colloquium on the Future of Legal Identity in April 2015, participants agreed that the term was directly linked to the right of recognition as stipulated within the Universal Declaration of Human Rights (UDHR), the Convention on the Rights of the Child (CRC) and the International Covenant on Civil and Political Rights (ICCPR).

jobs, were refused medical treatment, were blocked from accessing state welfare and were prevented from re-entering the country after travelling overseas.

While these examples illustrate the inherent risks that come with increasing the visibility of vulnerable populations (Hosein and Nyst, 2013), policymakers rarely examine the impact of contemporary legal identity practices on the 'users' of these systems particularly when these practices can give rise to disputes over questions of race, national identity and belonging.[12] Social protection programmes that reach domestic populations, for example, are regularly conceptualised at a macro-level from a desk in Washington rather than from the grassroots alongside practitioners in the field. Measures are therefore implemented 'without adequate (or any) consideration of the political, social or economic equilibrium with which [such] projects interact, and without serious consideration of the cost and benefit of such interventions' (Ladner et al., 2013, p. 4).

Social protection, while focusing on the inclusion of citizens, demands that beneficiaries are traceable and identifiable to the state and non-state actors. Social protection programmes that actively encourage the en masse registration of domestic populations have developed over a backdrop of vigilant security measures that manage, organise and track the individual. In the post–9/11 era, migrant-recipient nations are insisting that not only migrants but also increasingly citizens obtain their papers.[13] These measures have incremented the demands on states, particularly poorer nations with high emigration rates, to provide their nationals and transnational populations with identity documents. Bolstered by sophisticated datasets, improvements in technologies, administrative fees and quotas, and external donor support, states are developing systems that restrict the cross-border entry of migrants into sovereign terrain. In parallel to this, they have also been modernising state architectures, such as civil registries, so that they can more effectively manage the populations living within them (de Genova, 2018a, 2018b). This has happened alongside a rise in concerns over global securitisation and an interdependency on international legal frameworks. Through a focus on recent

---

12. Writing for the IADB, Mia Harbitz and Maria del Carmen Tamargo engage with these ideas but from the premise that gender and ethnicity can act as barriers to effective birth registration. They do not entertain the idea that states can also weaponise their own identification systems and use these to discriminate against populations on the basis of an individual's race, gender or ethnic origin. See M. Harbitz and M. del Carmen Tamargo, *The Significance of Legal Identity in Situations of Poverty and Social Exclusion: The Link between Gender, Ethnicity, and Legal Identity*, *Technical Note* (Washington, DC: IADB, 2009).

13. J. R. Varela, 'Trump's Immigration Plan Would Require Every Latino to Show Their Papers, Please', *Guardian*. 31 August 2015, https://www.theguardian.com/commentisfree/2015/aug/31/donald-trump-immigration-plan-would-require-every-latino-to-show-papers.

changes to immigration and citizenship laws and their impact on domestic populations, Parker asks whether we are experiencing a 'return to the local' (2015, p. 226) as we bear witness to a world in which not only migrants but increasingly citizens now find themselves the targets of discriminatory racial profiling and exclusionary practices.

Legal specialists and policymakers tend to assume that problems in accessing a legal identity stem from failures within the civil registry, such as an overly dogmatic bureaucracy, poorly trained staff, inefficient management or out-of-date technologies. This is why oftentimes the solution they propose to tackle under-registration is to further bolster the very systems that are exacerbating exclusion in the first place. As I will argue in this book, the development sector must be more sensitive to the racial, social and gender-specific tensions that can arise from formal identification practices particularly when these are prone to abuse and manipulation.

Birth Registration, Children and the Right to a Nationality

A birth certificate offers a 'passport to protection'[14] because it acts as a gateway to the exercise of fundamental rights. The widespread distribution of the birth certificate is popular with policymakers and NGOs who see it as a pragmatic and measurable way for states to evidence that they are meeting development targets. The document is a vital building block in the bureaucratic and administrative effectiveness of social policies as it provides legal specialists, development practitioners and academics with 'vital statistics'[15] that facilitate the collation of useful and accurate quantitative data. These statistics can bolster poverty reduction efforts including the efficient disbursement of welfare payments to ensure that financial assistance, such as conditional cash transfer (CCT) payments, reach targeted groups.

Legal identity through the issuance of a birth certificate cannot 'co-opt or compete with [the] state function [of granting citizenship]'. Nor can it 'recognise the details of an individual's birth or certify an individual's belonging to the polity' (Hunter and Brill, 2016, p. 197). These observations matter because despite the use of birth documentation to measure the successful implementation of the SDGs, a birth certificate does not necessarily determine a child's status as a national of the country where they are

---

14. UNICEF, *A Passport to Protection: A Guide to Birth Registration Programming* (New York: UNICEF, 2013).
15. P. Mahapatra, K. Shibuya, A. Lopez, F. Coullare, C. Chlapati Rao and S. Szreter., 'Civil Registration Systems and Vital Statistics: Successes and Missed Opportunities', *Lancet* 370, no. 9599 (2007): 1653–63.

born.[16] A baby, for example, might receive a birth document yet later as a teenager or adult finds that this document does not provide confirmation of their nationality. This can make it difficult for a young person to graduate from high school, obtain a passport or work in the formal economy.

The push for a universal legal identity is bringing the crisis of statelessness, and its effect on children born without their papers, to the global stage (van Waas, 2015). A stateless person is 'not considered a national by any state under the operation of its law'.[17] Birth documentation is therefore a useful tool in the fight against statelessness as it provides children with official recognition of their legal status from the moment they are born.[18]

The stateless have faced discrimination and ostracisation based on their national, religious and/or ethnic origins. Undocumented children and stateless populations are the target of legal identity measures as they are far more likely to experience socioeconomic hardship.[19] Without formal identification, it is difficult for the state and aid agencies to know where children are or identify their specific needs particularly if a child lives beyond the reaches of the formal economy and the social safety net.[20] Effective documentation therefore ensures that stateless populations, especially children, become more visible to the state, thus improving their access to education, healthcare and welfare. In the Global South, birth documentation can be particularly useful in rural areas where civil registries are hard to reach, mistakes recording birth dates and names are commonplace and burdensome financial requirements can impede the income-poor from ever regularising their status or that of their family members.

There are nevertheless problems with the assumption that universal birth registration will automatically ensure the social inclusion of all children.

---

16. In the United Kingdom, any person born to two foreign parents after 1983 – even when in possession of a state-issued birth certificate – is not automatically entitled to British citizenship. This change in the law was an important factor in the recent Windrush scandal, which involved a struggle between Black Anglophone Caribbeans and the British state to evidence their right to belong – as citizens – in the United Kingdom.
17. UNHCR, *The 1954 Convention Relating to the Status of Stateless Persons: Implementation within the European Union Member States and Recommendations for Harmonisation* (Geneva: UNHCR, 2003), 12.
18. UNHCR, 'UNHCR Action to Address Statelessness: A Strategy Note', *International Journal of Refugee Law* 22, no. 2 (2010): 297–335; UNHCR and Plan International, *Under the Radar and Under Protected: The Urgent Need to Address Stateless Children's Rights* (Woking, England/Geneva: UNHCR/Plan International, 2012).
19. The SDG for legal identity is measured via birth registrations.
20. C. Cody, *Count Every Child: The Right to Birth Registration* (Woking, England: Plan International, 2009).

Although birth certificates typically include information about a child's name and nationality,[21] they 'do not *confer* legal identity; they merely *confirm* it' (Vandenabeele, 2011, p. 307; emphasis in original). There are numerous reasons why a child might remain undocumented and therefore at risk of statelessness. In the case of migrant-descended populations, this can be due to a parent's restricted knowledge of citizenship laws, their lack of familiarity with state institutions and services, limited access to finances to pay for registrations and/or language problems (Manly et al., 2014). Civil registries have been prone to weak management especially when records are poorly archived, misplaced or destroyed (Hayes de Kalaf, 2015a, 2015b). A mother and/or father may find it difficult to access the civil registry if one or both parents have an irregular migratory status. Difficulties can also arise if an undocumented mother tries to register her child especially in countries where a father's nationality determines the legal status of his offspring.[22] This can be even more troublesome when informality is prevalent in the family across several generations as it can further complicate how a state determines a person's legal status.

Researchers are beginning to explore how emerging technologies and biometrics are exposing stateless persons, migrants and other noncitizens to human rights violations. Martínez and Wooding (2017), Achiume (2020), Weitzberg, Cheesman and Martin (2021), Manby (2020) and van der Straaten (2020) are already starting to develop robust intellectual frameworks that critically examine the impact of digital technologies on constructs of citizenship. This scholarship is becoming increasingly necessary as states work with big tech companies to roll out biometric systems (Lyon, 2009, pp. 135–51; Ajana, 2012, 2013). As the human rights specialist Bronwen Manby fittingly observes:

---

21. Some useful publications that focus on the right of children to birth registration include K. Apland, C. Hamilton, B. K. Blitz, M. Lagaay, R. Lakshman, and E. Yarrow, 'Birth Registration and Children's Rights: A Complex Story', Report of Coram Children's Legal Centre, 2015, https://www.planusa.org/docs/reports/2014-birth-registration-research-full-report.pdf; N. Perrault and A. Begoña, 'A Rights-Based Approach to Birth Registration in Latin America and the Caribbean', in *Challenges Newsletter. The Right to an Identity: Birth Registration in Latin America and the Caribbean* (Santiago de Chile: Economic Commission for Latin America and the Caribbean, 2011), 1–12; UNICEF, 'The Right to an Identity: Birth Registration in Latin America and the Caribbean' (Santiago de Chile: Economic Commission for Latin America and the Caribbean, 2011).

22. The overhaul of a political regime or changes in nationality law can create stateless populations. Gender bias within laws can also result in lineage passed down solely through the father or lost if a woman remarries. The arbitrary deprivation of citizenship is one of the major causes of statelessness and has received growing interest from scholarship in recent years.

There is near-universal consensus on the importance of 'legal identity' as a foundation for economic development and respect for rights. But insufficient attention is paid to the risks attendant on a drive to roll out biometric identification systems in fulfilment of this promise.[23]

Noting the limited empirical research that exists in this field beyond the birth registrations of children, we must consider the interconnectedness of contemporary registrations and the impact of these new technologies on the ways in which states are recording all of their citizens, including adults. This is necessary in the case of Latin America, where social policy has successfully hidden 'a reality of racist exclusion behind a mask of inclusiveness' (Wade, 2005, p. 239). As we will see in this book, as legal identity expanded, persons already in possession of valid ID documents and recognised within law as citizens began encountering real problems at the civil registry as state officials challenged or refused to acknowledge their legitimate claims to identity documentation.

Through a focus on citizenship-stripping practices and the experiences of (largely) Haitian-descended populations, I illustrate how international actors overlooked, ignored and downplayed the contestations that arose over who was allowed access to a legal identity. In the case of social policy, this is of particular import as noncitizens are typically ineligible for state benefits and find it harder to access healthcare, education, welfare and pensions (Cruz-Martínez, 2019). This book helps us consider some of the ways in which individuals are being categorised and included as citizens eligible for social protection and who, if anyone, is being left behind or excluded from these privileges.

Statelessness and the Dominican Case

The Dominican Republic has one of the highest levels of under-registration in Latin America and the Caribbean.[24] The country is home to the largest and most important case of statelessness in the Americas. After years of exhaustive study, this is the first book to examine the Dominican statelessness crisis and highlight the

23. B. Manby, '"Legal Identity" and Biometric Identification in Africa', *Migration and Citizenship: Newsletter of the American Political Science Association's Organized Section on Migration and Citizenship* 6, no. 2 (2018): 54.
24. This was the second highest under-registration rate in the region, followed by 19 per cent in both Haiti and Nicaragua, 15 per cent in Ecuador and 11 per cent in Jamaica. A. Pichardo Muñiz, 'Estudio Línea Base (ELB) y Evaluación del Impacto (EI) Proyecto de Inversión en la Protección Social (PIPS) de la República Dominicana. Informe Final Definitivo', Report by Gabinete de Coordinación de Políticas Públicas, Santo Domingo, 2012.

linkages between the promulgation of contemporary ID practices by international organisations with arbitrary measures that allowed the state to retroactively strip hundreds of thousands of Dominican-born (largely) Black Haitian-descended citizens of their citizenship. Disputes over whether Haitian-descended people should be recognised as Dominicans had been raging for years. Notwithstanding, the World Bank's insistence that the Dominican government implement large-scale legal identity measures to combat the under-registration of Dominicans created an opportunity for the country to permanently eliminate persons born to Haitians from the body politic.

For decades, the Dominican state had consistently failed to distinguish between Haitian migrants and their descendants arguing that children born to Haitian migrants were 'in transit' with no automatic right to Dominican citizenship (Ferguson, 2003, p. 335). In 2009, regional representatives gathered in La Romana in the south-east of the Dominican Republic[25] to attend the International Meeting of Civil Registry, Identity and Migration Administrators. Dominican state officials, while welcoming efforts to improve the registration of their own citizens, wanted to retain control over who it considered eligible for a Dominican identity. They were reluctant to acknowledge Haitian-descended people as citizens, including persons who had lived in the country for generations and already held a Dominican legal identity.[26] As one US embassy representative present at these discussions noted, even though the meeting was supposedly about the registration of Dominicans,

as soon as the doors closed on the public, the focus shifted decidedly to the 'Haitian' problem.[27]

Scholars see the Dominican case as a form of 'rooted' or 'in situ' displacement (Belton, 2015, pp. 907–21) which has rendered Dominican-born Haitian-descended populations 'legally stateless' (Bhabha, 2009; Bhabha and Robinson, 2011) due to their contested status and existence within law as citizens. Dominicans of Haitian descent experience a form of 'race-based statelessness' (Blake, 2014,

---

25. The fact this meeting was held in La Romana is significant. A popular tourist destination, it is also central to disagreements over access to documentation. It was the most important sugar-producing area in the country and is home to tens of thousands of Haitian migrants and their descendants.
26. K. Shipley, 'Stateless: Dominican-Born Grandchildren of Haitian Undocumented Immigrants in the Dominican Republic', *Transnational Law & Contemporary Problems* 20, no. 3 (2015): 459–87.
27. US Government Cable, *Dominicans Begin Work on Implementing Their 2004 Immigration Law* (Santo Domingo: US Government Cable, 2009a).

pp. 139–80) with undocumented nationals existing in limbo, living in a space between statelessness and citizenship (Hunter, 2019, pp. 37–47). Typically, these studies look to the two main geographical locations where the majority of undocumented and unregistered ('stateless') populations reside: the Haitian-Dominican border and/or the *batey*. These two important historical, cultural and ethnographic sites are helpful when examining the experiences of Haitian migrants together with those of their Dominican-born children. Nevertheless, the focus of this scholarship as an immigration 'problem' can unintentionally fail to address how the state retroactively used its state architectures to (re)define citizenship and facilitate the removal of its own citizens from the civil registry. This observation is central to the argument of this book because it pushes us to think more deeply about how the law and civil registry are used to purportedly legitimise practices that (re)construct, obstruct and challenge claims of Dominicans – not foreigners – to a legal identity.[28] We will see how Haitian-descended people had to fight the state to obtain and/or retain their documentation. Thousands more were rendered stateless by practices that refused to acknowledge their legal existence as citizens.

In the international development sector, identification systems are expanding rapidly with limited critique of how the large-scale registration of citizens might exacerbate exclusion for certain vulnerable and marginalised segments of the population. As we get closer to achieving the aim of universal legal identity, we need to be cautious about the potentially detrimental impact of these policies.[29]

In this chapter, I have argued that contemporary scholarship has neglected closer examination of the architectures that govern social policy initiatives and their impact on the en masse registration of populations (Hunter and Brill, 2016, p. 192). I have noted the importance of this in the lead-up to the 2030 SDGs, which are prioritising legal identity as a core aim. I have stated the importance of considering the interconnectedness of legal identity measures not solely on informal, unregistered or stateless children but also

---

28. While there are limited exceptions to this rule, before changes to the 2010 Dominican Constitution to abolish automatic birthright citizenship, Haitian-descended populations were born Dominican citizens. Some Dominican lawmakers continue to argue that since 1929 – the first year the 'in transit' definition appeared in the constitution – the state had erroneously recognised Haitian-descended populations as citizens and it was now rectifying this error. See J. M. Castillo Pantaleón, *La Nacionalidad Dominicana* (Santo Domingo: Editora Nacional, 2012).

29. G. Márquez, H. Berkman, C. Pagés, N. Gandelman, E. Gandelman, S. Calónico, V. Azevedo, M. Payne, J. C. Cárdenas, S. Duryea, J. C. Chaparro, E. Lora, H. R. Ñopo, J. Mazza, L. Ripani, A. F. Chong, S. Polanía, G. Márquez, C. P. Bouillon and G. León, *Outsiders? The Changing Patterns of Exclusion in Latin America and the Caribbean. 2008 Report* (Cambridge, MA: Harvard University Press, 2007).

on documented adults, including Black, Indigenous and migrant-descended populations already in possession of state-issued citizenship papers. I have also noted that scholars have yet to empirically examine in depth the ways in which contemporary legal identity policy, as presently promulgated by international organisations, might exacerbate discriminatory practices towards some groups. I suggest therefore that the Dominican case is particularly important as it involves people whom the state had already issued legal identity documentation, yet increasingly this group found their claims to national membership refuted by the Dominican authorities.

Chapter 2 introduces the specificities of the Dominican case, noting the limitations of existing methodological approaches that continue to examine questions of access to Dominican citizenship through the lens of Dominican-Haitian relations, cross-border migration and anti-Haitianism (*antihaitianismo*). Rather than see anti-Haitian hatred as the only rationale for the experiences of migrant-descended populations on the island, this book situates the Dominican case within a 'supra-national governmental regime in which the system of states, international agencies and multinational corporations play a fundamental role' (Hindess, 2002, pp. 129–30). In an attempt to shift our understandings of the Dominican case away from a singular focus on ethnocentricity and nationalism on the island (Thornton and Ubiera, 2019), this book places the experiences of Haitian-descended people within a broader, more relevant global context. In contrast to NGOs and scholars who interpret the difficulties the Haitian-descended are confronting as a migration 'problem' between the two countries, the chapter instead radically calls for us to *dehaitianise* contemporary approaches to the *Sentencia*. This is with the intention of being purposely provocative so that we can start to think about the far-reaching implications of legal identity practices across all populations. It is also to highlight the ambiguities and contradictions that can exist between state interpretations of our legal status and how we see ourselves. By instead looking at how state architectures can be used to challenge legitimate and existing claims to Dominican citizenship and the ways in which the state has used documentation and the civil registry to stop its own citizens from accessing paperwork, we can distance our approach away from an anti-Haitian, racist ideology that reinforces the perverse belief that persons of Haitian descent are somehow incompatible with the Dominican nation specifically because of their Black, African ancestry.

Chapter 3 traces the role of social policy in addressing under-registration in Latin America and the Caribbean over the past 30 years. I examine the expansion of contemporary social policy practices to illustrate how regional efforts to introduce structural adjustment reforms, improve subsidy spending and overhaul inefficient social programming became linked to efforts to increment rates of under-registration. I focus specifically on the involvement of inter-national actors such as the World Bank, the IADB and the United Nations to illustrate how the expansion of legal identity measures improved access to education and healthcare, the formal labour market, welfare, banking, financial services and voting for persons with the right ID. I examine the central role of CCTs – a widely implemented development strategy that targets, monitors and evaluates income-poor populations for welfare payments – in achieving this.[30] I argue that the CCT model has facilitated the marking of the income-poor and thus increased the visibility of vulnerable populations to the authorities. Through in-depth interviews with key actors in the international development sector and Dominican government representatives, I explore the problems that have emerged from these systems that insist upon the registra-tion and identification of all Indigenous and Afro-descended groups.

Chapter 4 provides a timeline of events leading up to the notorious 2013 *Sentencia* which arbitrarily stripped Juliana Deguis Pierre of her Dominican nationality. The chapter details how, since the 1990s, migrant rights groups began to strategically harness international support to advocate for the right of Dominican-born people of Haitian ancestry to a birth certificate and national ID card (*cédula de identidad y electoral*). I trace how Dominican and international NGOs working with Haitian migrants and their children used jurisprudence as both a domestic and a regional strategy to push the Dominican state to provide children of Haitian parentage with birth documentation. Campaign groups regularly equated a lack of birth certificates with a lack of nationality, arguing that without paperwork, children of Haitian ancestry could not access their Dominican legal identity and were therefore stateless. I illustrate how, in parallel to these policy measures, state officials began to introduce legal, bur-eaucratic and administrative mechanisms that increasingly blocked foreign-descended populations from accessing Dominican documentation from the civil registry. Although these measures affected undocumented, informal and stateless populations with no form of legal identity, they also began to impact individuals who were already registered as Dominican citizens. In this chapter, I interview key activists and NGO practitioners to better examine how tensions over access to a legal identity culminated in the 2013 *Sentencia* that retroactively invalidated the plaintiff Juliana Deguis Pierre's birth certifi-cate and made her stateless.

Chapter 5 amplifies the voices of documented persons of (largely) for-eign ancestry in the Dominican Republic. Through in-depth interviews, I demonstrate how citizens, as opposed to solely migrants, have increasingly

---

30. CCTs rely heavily on the need to document beneficiaries through the insistence that they provide a national identity card for inclusion onto social assistance programmes.

been forced to (re)navigate and (re)negotiate at times complex and cumbersome bureaucratic systems to (re)obtain their legal identity paperwork as Domincians. The chapter not only includes conversations with people still living in the Dominican Republic about their perceptions of identity and belonging but also considers the impact of foreign-making processes on transnational populations now based overseas. This is to highlight the far-reaching implications and unexpected consequences of legal identity measures – far beyond national borders.

Chapter 6 presents a summary of conclusions of the Dominican case. I argue that a critical analysis of the use of social policy to roll out legal identity measures is crucial over the coming decade as we head towards the 2030 SDGs. I call for greater scrutiny of social inclusion strategies and new technologies that aim to provide everyone, everywhere with some form of legal identity documentation. I ask that we consider the increasingly important role of digital identity in achieving these global aims. In the aftermath of the coronavirus pandemic, I underline the urgent need for more empirical research into the manufacturing of foreignness and the impact of these measures on citizens and their perceptions of identity and belonging.[31]

---

31. See M. Foster and J. Roberts, 'Manufacturing Foreigners: The Law and Politics of Transforming Citizens into Migrants', in *Research Handbook on the Law and Politics of Migration*, ed. Catherine Dauvergne (Northampton, MA: Elgar, 2021), 218–34.

Chapter 2

PERMANENTLY FOREIGN: HAITIAN-DESCENDED POPULATIONS IN THE DOMINICAN REPUBLIC

The idea is to link the cédula [national ID card] to our origins, our values, who we are as a nation. It is the document that identifies us.[1]

Bureaucracies were central to settler colonies, upholding the interests of dominant groups while systematically excluding domestic born populations from economic, political and social power (Parker, 2015) in the Americas. Settlers implemented numerous attempts to control Black and Indigenous bodies through the use of legal restrictions, registrations, vagrancy laws (Fisher and O'Hara, 2009), and the process of *blanqueamiento*, a means of social whitening which attempted to 'improve' the race of Latin Americans. Linked to ideas of modernity in post-colonial nations (Wade, 1993), *blanqueamiento* forged a Eurocentric identity via the creation of elaborate racial categorisation mechanisms that favoured whites and foreigners over Indigenous and Afro-descended groups, the income-poor and women.

The island of Hispaniola, shared between Haiti and the Dominican Republic, was pivotal to the bureaucratic and economic expansion of the Americas (Gómez Nadal, 2017). Since the colonial era, the island has been closely connected to globalisation and the movement of peoples (Mintz, 1966, pp. 289–331; Chamberlain, 1998, p. 1). It long 'predate[d] the modern' (Mintz and Price, 1985; Howard, 2017), playing an important role in the world economy and capitalist expansion. Plantation-based labour was the driving force of this colonial project which forcibly and brutally removed hundreds of thousands of people from West Africa to exploit under slavery.

White colonialism demanded Black conformity to this world system, preventing any form of agency in an attempt to destroy the Black man's sense

---

1. Original quote from Roberto Rosario Márquez, director of the Dominican civil registry: 'La idea es vincular la cédula a nuestros orígenes, a nuestros valores, lo que somos como nación, porque es el documento de identificación.' *Listín Diario, Rosario dice nueva cédula incluirá escudo de la bandera y será expresión de la dominicanidad*, Santo Domingo, 2014.

of self (Fanon, 1952). In the West, French colonial powers profited hand-somely from sugar plantation agriculture imposed in Haiti in the eighteenth century while subjecting slaves to rape, torture and extreme physical and psychological exhaustion.

Emerging from this brutal and repressive environment, the slaves fought back. A pivotal event in world history, the Haitian Revolution (1791–1804) represented an 'upside-down world' (San Miguel, 2005, p. 22) in which African slaves disrupted the global order by fighting and ultimately ousting the European colonisers occupying the island. Significantly, the Haitian Revolution resulted in the formation of the first free Black republic. This mass rebellion – both a radical and an unthinkable act (James, 1938; Trouillot, 1991) – sent shock waves throughout the world specifically because Haitians demanded that Blacks be free to rule and self-govern away from the clutches of white colonial settlers.

Against a backdrop of revolution and resistance in neighbouring Haiti, the Dominican Republic became an 'imperial backwater' (Roorda, 1998, p. 7). Abandoned by Spanish settlers who left for Central America in search of gold and greater wealth (Moya Pons, 2009), the country experienced labour exploitation to a much lesser degree of intensity than Haiti. Instead it became a 'backward agrarian society' model (Abel and Lewis, 2015, p. 339) relying on subsistence farming and hunting. The Dominican identity rests within this specific colonial history where racial mixing was far more prevalent than in Haiti (San Miguel, 1997; Torres-Saillant, 1998; Candelario, 2000). To exert political and economic control over the poor majority, the intellectual elite spread fear about the threat of a Haitian invasion into Dominican territory.[2] They drew on the post-revolutionary efforts of Haitians to abolish slavery across the whole island, as well as the subsequent Haitian occupation of the Dominican Republic (1822–44), to instil fear into the Dominican people about the dangers of racial, cultural and linguistic mixing with Haitians.

Antihaitianimo, Blackness and Haiti

Historically, the Dominican state has marked persons of Haitian ancestry with a form of 'permanent foreignness'.[3] Haitian-descended populations, once

---

2. Former authoritarian president Joaquin Balaguer (1957–60, 1960–62, 1966–78, 1986–96) reiterated these concerns in his book, *La Isla al Revés: Haití y el Destino Dominicano* (1985). He shared fears with other prominent intellectual nationalists, such as Peña-Batlle and Demorizi, that the Dominican nationality could eventually disintegrate in the face of increased migration from Haiti.
3. These concerns are shared by the Dominican scholar Silvio Torres-Saillant. He reminds us that the mingling together of foreigners with Dominicans is exceptional only in the

born with the *jus soli* right to a Dominican nationality, are often referred to as *haitianos* (Haitians) or *haitianos de aquí* (Haitians from here). These terms are regularly applied to people who have lived in the Dominican Republic over several generations, who have never travelled to or rarely visit Haiti and who speak Spanish, rather than Haitian *kreyòl*, as their mother tongue. At times, *haitiano* is used to label Black Dominicans as non-belongers, even if they have no Haitian or other immediate foreign ancestry.

With the support of the Catholic Church, the state enforced a racially motivated Eurocentric doctrine known as *antihaitianismo* (anti-Haitianism). The ruling elite deployed *antihaitianismo* as an ideological and repressive tool which negated, downplayed and discarded Blackness, associating this with Africa, savagery and non-belonging. A brutal ideology, *antihaitianismo* was employed to emphasise a 'white', Catholic, Hispanic Dominican identity over the Haitian 'other' (Howard, 2001; Sagás, 2002). The Dominican elite used *antihaitianismo* to celebrate the 'imagined' (Anderson, 1983; San Miguel, 1997) Europeanness of the Dominican people and its perceived racial superiority over that of its neighbour.

By the twentieth century the Dominican Republic relied increasingly on Haitian migrant labour to develop a profitable sugar industry. Haitian migrants remained in the country over the course of several decades. There they had children and grandchildren. Many did not settle through choice. Instead, they were brought by sugar companies and forced to work in deplorable conditions, living in isolation from Dominicans. These practices created 'states of exception' (Agamben, 1995) which physically and geographically separated migrants and their children from everyday contact with Dominicans. These rural plantation enclaves are known as *bateyes* and are the '*kilómetro zero* [*sic*] (ground zero) of debates' on race and belonging (Mayes, 2014). The *batey* is therefore a site of great ethnographic importance for researchers looking at the lives of Haitian migrants and their experiences of statelessness.

Life for the Haitian-descended was different along the border. Although contractual labour did exist, Haitians and Dominicans regularly interacted

case of Haiti. In a scholarly conversation on recent events, he notes how the Dominican political elite recognises persons of Italian and other foreign parentage resident in the country for several generations as Dominicans. He laments that the state fails to apply the same logic to Dominicans of Haitian ancestry in a way that marks this group with a form of 'permanent foreignness'. Original quote: 'En otras palabras, predomina un discurso que condena a los dominicanos de herencia haitiana a la extranjeridad permanente.' This quote was made in the article 'Me atemorizan los planes de Leonel Fernández para con la diáspora' by the online newspaper acento.com.do. S. Torres-Saillant, 2015. https://acento.com.do/actualidad/silvio-torres-saillant-me-atemorizan-los-planes-de-leonel-fernandez-para-con-la-diaspora-8250040.html.

with one another, transiting the largely unregulated and porous perimeter. While many Haitian labourers and their relatives returned to live in Haiti each day, others began to settle in the Dominican Republic and have children there. The border allowed Haitians and Dominicans to integrate more freely, forming kinship ties, friendships and families (Eller, 2016; Mayes and Jayaram, 2018). The settlement of Haitians, and the rising number of Haitian-descended people born in the country, began to concern a fiercely anti-Haitian political elite. Nationalists did not like the lack of control they had over the cross-border mixing of Haitians and Dominicans. The widespread interaction of Haitians and Dominicans at the border contrasted with life in the *batey*, where the state and international sugar companies continued to restrict the movements of Haitians and their engagement with outsiders.

The government began carrying out investigations in the *bateyes* to determine just how many Haitian-descended people were living in the country. They talked about Haitians and their descendants interchangeably, failing to distinguish between the two groups. In their reports, state officials shared concerns about the number of Haitian migrants living, settling and procreating in the Dominican Republic, the 'shifting, complex or ambiguous identities [of whom were] [...] perceived as a problem for the state' (Turits, 2002, p. 593), For nationalists, it was precisely because Haitian-descended populations living on the border could be mistaken for Dominicans, could speak Spanish and were seemingly assimilating into Dominican society that they represented such a great threat to the cultural fabric of the nation. As one official reported:

> although these people seem harmless, they think like Haitians, they live like Haitians, and they act like Haitians. [...] [If] any disagreement takes place between the two countries, they will favor their relatives and countrymen, to the detriment of our territorial integrity and the Dominican people.[4]

This was not the first time the Dominican state had tried to address its 'Haitian problem'. During the dictatorship of Rafael Leónidas Trujillo Molina (1930–61), 'fantasies of race and class mobility' penetrated every aspect of Dominican life (Derby, 2009, p. 7). In 1937, Trujillo attempted to put an end to cross-border racial mixing by 'Dominicanizing' the country through the violent slaughter of tens of thousands of Dominican border dwellers. In his attempt to exert political control at the border and to safeguard the Dominican

---

4. A. Hintzen, *Cultivating Resistance: Haitian-Dominican Communities and the Dominican Sugar Industry, 1915–1990* (Coral Gabes, FL: University of Miami, 2016), 224.

Republic from what he considered the cultural, linguistic and racial Haitian 'threat' of Blackness, Trujillo ordered the massacre of tens of thousands of 'Haitians' living in the region. Although the massacre is largely thought of as an attack against Haitians, those murdered died precisely because their Blackness made them appear 'foreign' and therefore non-Dominican (Paulino, 2015) to the machete-wielding soldiers.

In an attempt to distance himself from his own Haitian heritage,[5] Trujillo used the construct of the imagined indigeneity[6] of the Dominican nation as a means to underpin a national project that aligned the people with their former Spanish colonisers (San Miguel, 2005). The state employed the myth and ambiguity of the *indio/a* to explain the racial mixing of the Dominican people via the creation of a new racial category that was neither Black nor white. The construct of the *indio/a* was useful to nationalists as it provided Dominicans with a way to self-identify as something other than Black.

As the historian Amelia Hintzen has shown us, in the 1930s Trujillo introduced the country's first national identity card, the *cédula*. The national ID card, used as a means to identify a person's 'Haitian-ness' to the authorities (Hintzen, 2016, pp. 96, 272), stated the place of residence and the skin colour of the card bearer. This allowed the state to implement an 'appearance-based system of description' (Wheeler, 2015, p. 36) which racially classified individuals at the discretion of a government official.

The inclusion of the *indio* classification on the national ID was a strategy used to purge the African origins of the Dominican people away from the national conscience. Usage of the term *indio* meant that a civil registry official could classify a card bearer's dark complexion, helping explain why a wealthier Dominican might 'look' Black while at the same time seemingly justifying why they could never *be* Black. Conversely, the term *negro* was applied to poorer populations, including the Haitian-descended. The construct of the *indio* was therefore used to psychologically distance people from their Black roots, allowing Dominicans to ignore their origins as the descendants of enslaved Africans, an association which brought them closer to Haiti (Eller, 2016).

---

5. Trujillo's grandmother was said to be Haitian. Before appearing in public, Trujillo would whiten his appearance with face powder and strongly denied any connection with Haiti. See R. D. Crassweller, *Trujillo: The Life and Times of a Caribbean Dictator* (New York: Macmillan, 1966).
6. Most Indigenous people on the island, including the Taínos, were exterminated shortly after the arrival of Christopher Columbus. Some were killed by force due to enslavement although many also succumbed to the diseases brought by the Spaniards, such as influenza, smallpox and typhus.

The Identification of Haitian-Descended Populations

To learn more about recent controversies over access to citizenship in the country, I spoke with the Dominican journalist and human rights activist Juan Bolívar Díaz, who has been highly critical of identification measures on the island. Bolívar Díaz writes regularly for the national newspaper *Hoy* on the systematic exclusion of Dominicans of Haitian descent from the Dominican civil registry. He told me:

> We [Dominicans] are Blacks and we are Spanish. We're not Indians. We don't have Indians. We use the term *indio* to say we are not Black. Those who are in the minority are the whites. There are not just *mulattos*[7] but Blacks. Many people who are *mulattos* think that they are white. That's until they arrive in Europe or the US and they realise they are not as white as they had initially thought.[8]

Bolívar Díaz talked to me about racial mixing and the trauma associated with the Dominican identity. The *mulatto*, he argued, was not the product of love between two people but was born from rape. The white Spaniard, the slave owner, the coloniser, the oppressor had systematically abused the Black woman to express his primitive and macho needs, he told me. This is why, he reasoned, the Dominican male does not accept his Black identity. A Dominican cannot be a *negro* or *mulatto* but instead seeks to find acceptance as an *indio* or white man:

> There is racial hatred. It is about revenge. Revenge against the Blacks who have invaded the country. Not because we have exploited them for decades with low wages and terrible conditions [sarcastic tone]. They invaded us(!) [laughs] Some things make no sense. Errors have happened. Mistakes have been made. *Dominicanidad* [Dominicanness] is an elastic term. A Dominican doesn't recognise himself. We have no racial or cultural identity if we deny the Black component in our blood, our culture.

Dominicanness (*dominicanidad*) emerged as the antithesis of the Haitian identity (Howard, 2001, pp. 5, 41), which, for nationalists, posed a grave threat to the future of the nation. Paradoxically, women were seen as both the

---

7. The use of the term 'mulatto' is common in Dominican vernacular. It means a person of mixed race born to one Black and one white parent.
8. This quote is from an interview with the Dominican journalist Juan Bolívar Díaz on 27 August 2016.

incubators of this feared invasion and standing at the frontline of efforts to defend the Dominican bloodline. Demonised for their sexual relationship with Haitians, women who procreated with Haitian men were accused of allowing their foreign-descended children to enter the body politic as Dominican citizens. In response to the growing number of Haitian-descended children born and settling in the Dominican Republic, in 1969 the Director of Migration Manuel de Jesús Estrada Medina requested a solution to this 'problem'. He stated:

> [Haitians] have been procreating with Dominican mothers who – because they were born here – are Dominicans – something which is contributing to [an] invasion at an alarming rate, and therefore constitutes a real and positive threat to our nationality.[9]

A close ally of Trujillo, the authoritarian leader Joaquin Balaguer made use of the large numbers of undocumented Dominican, Haitian and Haitian-descended populations living in rural areas during election periods to his strategic advantage. In spite of his fervent anti-Haitian stance, in the 1970s he purposely targeted migrant-heavy locations in an effort to hand out identity documentation to Haitian migrants and their Dominican-born descendants as a means to secure votes for his party. This political play was enormously beneficial to the state as it used voting systems and the Dominican national ID card as a means to provide legitimacy to a corrupt and authoritarian regime that was desperate to hold on to power at any cost.

I met with a former World Bank employee Samuel Carlson, who in the next chapter talks in detail about the growing involvement of international development organisations in the registrations of the Dominican population. Carlson understood the value of the national identity card and that the state had strategically used it for political and economic gain. He told me:

> Historically, Balaguer had issued *cédulas* [Dominican identity cards] to tens of thousands of people who then voted for him. Even when many people thought they were Haitians [...] they [government officials] went to the communities and gave the [Dominican] *cédula* away. It was easy to

---

9. A. J. Petrozziello, A. Hintzen and J. C. González Díaz, 'Memorandum to President Balaguer from the Director of Migration, 1969', in *Género y el riesgo de apatridia para la población de ascendencia haitiana en los bateyes de la República Dominicana* (Santo Domingo: Centro para la Observación Migratoria y el Desarrollo en el Caribe, 2014), 208–10.

get hold of. People would turn up on trucks and give out documents to anybody. One *cédula* equalled one vote.

By handing out papers, Balaguer ensured that both Dominicans and Haitians could participate in elections, even when many were not formally registered. He purposely gave papers to undocumented Haitians so that they could vote for his party as Dominicans. As the state began to modernise and 'clean up' its civil registry, people who once had documents given to them by the authorities subsequently found that their details were either not recorded or could not be found within the civil registry. They encountered these difficulties precisely because the Dominican ruling elites had haphazardly provided them with their paperwork without ever formally registering their details.

By the 1980s, the state began to rely less and less on manual labour from its Haitian neighbour. The Dominican sugar industry had reached a slump with the economy in slow decline. Human rights abuses against Haitians and their families were commonplace. The police and military would stop and search anyone they could claim might 'appear' Haitian or foreign. Undocumented migrants and Haitian-descended populations suffered the most at the hands of these practices. Many would find themselves challenged while travelling on public transport and asked to provide a copy of their Dominican ID. Through a lack of access to official documentation, the descendants of Haitian migrants were restricted to the *batey* 'in social status as well as territorial space' (Derby, 2009, p. 159). At times, persons of Haitian ancestry, even when in possession of a valid Dominican identity card,[10] would be arbitrarily expulsed across the border.[11] Others were unable to leave the plantations because they had no paperwork at all.

These practices, however, did not solely affect Haitians and their immediate descendants. The police would also challenge Black Dominicans for proof of legal status. As we will see in the interviews in Chapter 5, this included *cocolo*-descended populations who had travelled to the Dominican Republic from the Anglophone, Francophone and Dutch Caribbean.[12] This observation matters because regardless of the papers these

---

10. See J. Ferguson, 'Migration in the Caribbean: Haiti, the Dominican Republic and Beyond', *Minority Rights Group International* (2003).

11. A state can deport migrants and expulse citizens; hence I use the term 'expulsion' as opposed to 'deportation' when talking about the Haitian-descended.

12. *Cocolos* is a term used to describe Afro-descended populations originating from the Anglophone, Francophone and Dutch Caribbean. Tens of thousands of *cocolos* migrated to Samaná in the north-east, Puerto Plata on the north coast and San Pedro de Macorís in the east. Many worked in the sugar industry and in ports in the late nineteenth century. This wave of migration was later replaced by the introduction of Haitian labour as a cheaper and more labour-intensive alternative. We will learn more about this group in Chapter 5.

individuals had on their person, officials would often question or ignore their legitimacy if the documents belonged to persons of African and/or Haitian origin.[13] It did not matter whether a Dominican citizen possessed a valid ID, the police and military would still use the national identity card as a means to intimidate, harass, deport and expulse people.

The election of Leonel Fernández to the Partido de la Liberación Dominicana (Dominican Liberation Party, PLD) presidency in 1996 marked a new era of democratisation and political and economic reform (Mitchell, 2014). A key dynamic in this ascension to power was a deal that the PLD brokered with the ultra-nationalist, anti-Haitian Fuerza Nacional Progresista (National Progressive Force, FNP). In joining forces, the PLD and the FNP implemented an electoral coalition to launch a racist hate campaign against the candidacy of José Francisco Peña Gómez to the Dominican presidency. Peña Gómez was born to Haitian parents and adopted by a Dominican peasant family after his parents fled during the 1937 massacre. His popularity with the masses scared the fiercely anti-Haitian Dominican elite particularly as he was a powerful Black intellectual who embodied the antithesis of how they conceptualised the national identity. The racism unleashed against Peña Gómez in the mid-1990s resulted in a newly repressive turn during which time there were workplace and neighbourhood raids as well as mass deportations of Haitian migrants across the border.

The actions of the Dominican military received considerable attention from human rights organisations at this time who reacted strongly to these overt displays of aggression, state violence and discrimination. By the mid-2000s, the government had committed to improving the registration of Dominicans as a way of facilitating the more accurate implementation of measures to take poor Dominicans out of structural poverty.[14] Fernández nevertheless remained highly dependent on the old paternalistic institutions of his predecessors. On the one hand, he was eager to appease international funders and demonstrate the country was reducing excessive spending and improving its poor human rights record. On the other, he had to mediate resistance from domestic actors, particularly a powerful nationalist faction within the PLD that was strongly opposed to any attempts

---

13. See Robert F. Kennedy Human Rights (American Jewish World Service, Centro de Desarrollo Sostenible, the United Nations Democracy Fund), *Dreams Deferred: The Struggle of Dominicans of Haitian Descent to Get Their Nationality Back* (Washington, DC, 2017).
14. F. Regalia and M. Robles, *Social Assistance, Poverty and Equity in the Dominican Republic, Economic and Sector Study Series* (Washington, DC: Inter-American Development Bank, 2005).

to provide the Haitian-descended with Dominican citizenship documentation and recognise them as contributors to the formal economy.

As the demand for formalised labour increased, so did requests for identity papers. The Dominican national identity card became a necessary route to formal employment as it was required to carry out a gamut of rudimentary and administrative tasks. I spoke with one anonymous NGO worker who told me:

> There is a problem with documentation in the country. There is a large number of people who do not have their paperwork. Both Dominicans and foreigners. The JCE [civil registry] doesn't give out answers. There is a bureaucratic *tollo* [mess]. There are a lot of lost opportunities. Now you need a *cédula* to get a job here. You need it for health insurance, to work in a free trade zone, to study. If not [...] if you need to travel [...] what are you going to do? Everyone asks you for a document.

Social policy became extremely useful for the Dominican government because it was a helpful way of avoiding unwelcome exposure regarding the country's mistreatment of Haitians and their children. It meant the government could focus on the social inclusion of income-poor Dominicans into the formal economy. International actors and the government could then centre discussions on the identification of Dominican populations to improve the disbursement of state welfare, effectively bypassing any mention of discriminatory practices against Haitian migrants or their children. The discourse instead hinged on a discussion of social inclusion, not arbitrary exclusion.

Nevertheless, many were starting to encounter problems with registrations, particularly young adults. In our interview, an NGO practitioner highlighted this by stating:

> Most young people who do not have documents don't leave their community. They don't have anywhere to go. Sometimes with a piece of paper they can move around without their *cédula* [ID card]. But this is changing. If you're the same colour as me, they stop you. If you don't have your document, they send you back to your house or they send you to Haiti without you knowing where you're going. [...] I have seen a lot of young people. They take away their nationality. The ID does not say that they are Dominicans. It says that they are the children of foreigners. They are irregular. There is one ID that says they are foreigners. This is for people born abroad but they give it to them [people born in the Dominican Republic]. They are not happy about this. They can't do what they wanted to do. They can't have access to credit or borrow

money. They don't enjoy things in the same way. They should have given these people their *cédula*. They are from here.

The ethnographer Simmons illustrates very clearly some of the contradictions and contestations that can arise when Black Dominicans try and obtain their ID. In an ethnographic study of the Dominican civil registry (JCE), Simmons observes how government officials used registration practices to (re)construct their own interpretations of race (2009, pp. 48–49). She examines how a civil registry official records the racial classification of a man for his national identity card. She recounts how, with each attempt to capture this information, the computer freezes. On three separate occasions, the official takes a different photograph of the man. On the first try, she changes his skin colour on the computer from *indio* to *negro*. After restarting her machine, she then records his *indio* status as *mulatto*. On the third attempt, she switches the classification back again from *indio* to *negro*. After consulting with her supervisor, the official eventually decides to leave the *indio* status unchanged. Within this one process, Simmons shows how, unbeknownst to the man, two different state officials intervened to register and re-register their own versions of his racial categorisation. This was based entirely on their own interpretation of how his Blackness interacted with their perception of his Dominicanness.

To help me understand the impact of contemporary legal identity measures on populations of Haitian ancestry, I spoke with Arsénito Santana, a health worker from the NGO Centre for Sustainable Development (CEDESO) in Tamayo, a small town in the southwest of the country. I also spoke with Yoni Tusen[15] and Midouard Confident, who worked at 180° for Cooperation and Development, a Spanish NGO in La Romana (Figure 1), the most important sugar-producing area in the Dominican Republic, which has experienced high levels of Haitian and Anglo-Caribbean migration. The town was used as a 'testing ground' to roll out the new registrations and in recent years has also become a popular tourist destination.

Santana and Tusen were both of Haitian descent. Confident was a Haitian who lived and worked in Dominican sugar cane plantation communities: the batey (Figure 2). All three men cared deeply about the impact of registrations on their friends and families and expressed a commitment to helping affected people overcome documentation problems. CEDESO fieldworker Santana had grown up in a batey and initially described himself to me as

---

15. The names Tusen and Toussaint are common among Haitian-descended populations living in the Dominican Republic. They refer to François-Dominique Toussaint Louverture, leader of the Haitian revolution (1791–1804).

Figure 1 Train transporting sugar cane on a Dominican batey in La Romana. Credits: author.

the *hijo de haitianos* (the son of Haitians). It was only after we had talked for a number of hours did it transpire that he was in fact a fourth-generation Haitian. He had lived in the Dominican Republic all his life, as had his parents and grandparents. When I asked why he had said his parents were migrants, he was surprised. He responded: 'Coño, sí. ¡Tienes razón!' ('Bloody hell, yes. You're right!'). He then laughed and talked about how absurd he found the whole situation, stating:

> I am a Dominican but to them [the elite] I won't ever really be one.

My conversations with Santana highlighted the ambiguities associated with registrations and the increasing importance of the identity card. People, he told me, have grown up as Dominicans, yet the state sees them as migrants. This has affected the movement of Haitian-descended populations within the country and had an impact on their access to services. The three men said that young people living in the bateyes had heard about the *Sentencia* on the radio and through their neighbours. There was a lack of clarity and widespread

Figure 2 Batey 8 near La Romana. Credits: author.

confusion. People would stop them in the street and ask for their help. They observed how these practices were affecting communities in haphazard ways. Significantly, they did not understand why they had their documentation when others were struggling:

> I don't know why this did not affect me. My cousin, my neighbours, a young lad in the community I studied with. I see them affected. These are people born in the community. You feel empathy for them. I see problems in the future. They need to sort this out. They [the JCE] gave them the documents so that they had something in their hand. But it should not say *residente permanente* ('permanent resident'). They were born in the country and they deserve to be treated better.

Tusen told me that NGOs would pay to transport groups of people trying to get their papers. Despite the communications campaigns, there was a lack of information. In the past, people had been allowed to have a lawyer accompany them and argue their case with registry officials. Now, this had all changed. People living in rural areas were confused by the procedures. It was clear that the three men cared deeply about what was happening and saw this as a grave injustice. They had heard complaints from both Dominicans and Haitians about their interactions with the state and the difficulties they were facing in securing their documents:

> They [the state] tell them [the Haitian-descended] they are not Dominicans. In Haiti, they say they are not Haitians. Do they feel Haitian? Do they identify as Haitians? No. No. Can you imagine? They don't know the culture, the environment. It is not the same thing. They have no *patria* [homeland]. They are going to take them to a country they do not know. Where am I going to go? Where do I have to go if my mum and dad are here?

The journalist Bolívar Díaz considered the treatment of the Haitiandescended a form of bureaucratic violence. In contrast to international organisations, NGOs and fieldworkers who have focused their energies on the right of children and young people born to Haitian migrants to birth documentation, he asked why so much energy was being put into insisting that all people now had their paperwork. This made no sense for older people, particularly the income-poor living in rural areas. He reasoned that this group rarely got formally married, and they had little need for divorce papers or other documents such as a passport. He stated:

> What do they [the elderly] need these documents for? They don't need a birth certificate. These people were excluded but in practice many still have some form of documentation.

Bolívar Díaz said that heightened scrutiny of people's records had affected individuals born in the Dominican Republic over three or four generations. He maintained that although this group had its origins in Haiti, culturally, linguistically and psychologically they were Dominicans. He also noted the transnational implications of these measures, underlining that some people struggling to renew their documents had now left the island and were living overseas. We will hear more about the impact of legal identity measures on people's lived experiences in Chapter 5.

A Call to Dehaitianise Approaches to the Dominican Case

Claims over who has the right to recognition as a Dominican are fraught with ambiguities specifically because the Dominican identity is consistently being (re)defined and (re)imagined. It is rooted in a complex history of settler-colonial rule, forced labour and the systematic erasure of Blackness. Shape-shifting and contradictory, the construct of *dominicanidad* has often depended 'on the agenda of the identifier' (Perez Hazel, 2014, p. 80), manipulated by those in power for political or financial gain. In addition, some Dominicans self-identify in conflicting ways, negating their own African roots as a means to align themselves more closely with whiteness. If we think more critically about how the Dominican identity exists, changes and is experienced at a legal, social and personal level, we can more readily challenge the ways in which the Dominican state is weaponising the question of state membership as an assault against its own people.

Unquestionably, anti-Haitian sentiment is a central and fundamental factor in explaining the discriminatory actions of the Dominican state against Haitian-descended populations. I am being intentionally provocative when I suggest that we *dehaitianise* approaches to this case. This is neither to detract from this discrimination nor to diminish the importance of existing scholarship on *antihaitianismo*, statelessness or migration. Instead, I am arguing that there is a need to move away from oversimplified, binary interpretations of this crisis as an anomalous domestic 'immigration' dispute between the Dominican Republic and its Haitian neigbour. This places an overwhelming emphasis on the foreignness and non-belonging of affected populations, namely, documented Dominican citizens who, from birth, have had a legitimate and existing claim to state membership. A focus on fervent anti-Haitian nationalism, Haitian migration into the country and bi-national relations between the two countries fails to consider the influence of global actors in exacerbating disputes over access to citizenship on the island. This sadly then flattens the experiences of people who have grown up in the country and consider it their home. We will examine the importance of this in greater depth in the next chapter.

By *dehaitianising* our framing of this case, we can instead begin to construct a new discourse that emphasises the social inclusion and belonging of Dominicans. In an effort to acknowledge these contradictions and to steer the debate in new directions, Lorgia García-Peña (2016) helpfully and radically re-envisions the Dominican identity as a form of empowerment. Rather than replicate Dominicanness as an elite construct that is implicitly anti-Haitian or argue the complex legal case for why Haitian-descended populations should be treated as Dominican citizens, she emphasises the right of all Dominicans, including persons of Haitian ancestry and Dominican-descended populations living overseas, to take ownership of the term. García-Peña sees this reclaiming important for individuals who culturally, linguistically and emotionally see themselves as Dominicans regardless of how the state or other actors may interpret or record their legal status. As she suggests, this would allow us to celebrate the multiple ways in which Dominicans self-identify and the important and positive contributions their national and ethnic origins have contributed to how they perceive and understand their own construct of Dominicanness.

This approach then gives us space to think in more nuanced and multifaceted ways about how the state constructs an identity that oftentimes conflicts with people who see themselves as Dominicans, regardless of how the state identifies them. It broadens up our analysis of belonging to other locations, so that we not only look to affected populations living along the border or in the *batey* but also consider new geographical locations and lived experiences, including those of the Dominican diaspora living overseas (Sagás, 2018). As Aber and Small rightly observe, this new thinking is important specifically because citizenship-stripping practices not only affect children but also inevitably have an impact across the entire population. They are inextricably interconnected with one another.

> When policies motivated by anti-Haitianism are implemented, the negative impacts are felt by all people who are somehow marked as Haitian, regardless of whether they are recent migrants, third generation Dominicans or even black Dominicans with no Haitian ancestry. Anti-Haitianism destabilizes the citizenship system, as well as broader senses of membership and belonging. (2013, p. 8)

In the next chapter, we will examine how the Dominican state used its social policy sector to roll out large-scale legal identity programmes in alignment with global policy. We will begin to hear from international development specialists, Dominican government officials and Haitian-descended populations about their experiences of legal identity practices. We will see how the World Bank in particular, although aware of the potential for problems with migrant-descended populations in (re)obtaining their papers, continued to fund the Dominican government's efforts to provide all persons they were choosing to identify as Dominicans with a legal identity. This led to practices that facilitated the administrative (re)ordering of Dominican citizens, resulting in the bureaucratic erasure of Haitian-descended populations from the country's civil registry.

Chapter 3

INCLUDING THE 'EXCLUDED': INTERNATIONAL ORGANISATIONS AND THE ADMINISTRATIVE (RE)ORDERING OF DOMINICANS

[In the DR] [...] the pendulum swung so far that it became nearly impossible to get your [legal identity] documents if your parents did not have an ID card.[1]

Today, policymakers see Latin America and the Caribbean as a triumph in the global fight against under-registration. Governments have successfully halved the number of undocumented births,[2] helping bring marginalised 'outsiders' within the reach of the formal economy and the social safety net (Garay, 2016). As we saw in Chapter 1, the 'administrative ordering' (Scott, 1998) of populations through the improvement of civil registries has become a fundamental component of global social policy. Over the past three decades, international actors have incorporated legal identity as a core cross-cutting theme.[3] The region is now on track to achieve the global UN Sustainable Development Goal (SDG) of universal birth registration by 2030.[4]

In this chapter, I illustrate how the World Bank's involvement in sponsoring and enforcing legal identity exacerbated historical tensions over the right of Haitian-descended populations born in the country to a Dominican nationality.

---

1. Samuel Carlson, former World Bank employee.
2. C. Dunning, A. Gelb and S. Raghavan, 'Birth Registration, Legal Identity, and the Post-2015 Agenda', Center for Global Development, CGD Policy, 2014, 5–6.
3. N. Perrault and A. Begoña, 'A Rights-Based Approach to Birth Registration in Latin America and the Caribbean', in *Challenges Newsletter. The Right to an Identity: Birth Registration in Latin America and the Caribbean* (Santiago de Chile: Economic Commission for Latin America and the Caribbean, 2011), 4–9.
4. UNICEF, *Progress for Children: A World Fit for Children – Statistical Review* (New York: UNICEF, 42).

Although for years the authorities had informally refused to issue the Haitian-descended with their documents, I show how these problems intensified as efforts to modernise the civil registry and provide a universal legal identity expanded. International organisations, aware of disputes over access to citizenship as well as the sensitivities around questions of race and national belonging on the island, continued to fund and push for the expansion of these citizenship-stripping practices, ultimately dismissing the experiences of people as a sovereign matter for the Dominican authorities to address.

The Under-Registration of Afro-Descended and Indigenous Populations in the Americas

The international debt crisis of the 1980s had a significant impact on spending power, incomes and unemployment levels. To address the burgeoning crisis, the World Bank and the International Monetary Fund (IMF) renegotiated lending and introduced structural adjustment loans to promote the integration of neo-liberal policies in the Americas.[5] The regional governments that accepted these conditions subsequently prioritised deficit reduction over investment in human capital and infrastructure. This lack of social spending created a 'lost decade' in development,[6] which had an overly harmful impact on the poor.

Over this time, an ideological shift in social policy began to take place. This moved from a sole preoccupation with economic reforms to the introduction of structural adjustment policies that involved a more integrated focus on human capabilities.[7] International funders began to harmonise efforts away from the prioritisation of economic prosperity to ensure that all populations were shielded from the impact of extreme poverty.[8] As a result of these debates, multilateral organisations implemented a series of initiatives that placed the poor at the very centre of social policy.[9]

---

5. World Bank, *World Development Report 2004: Making Services Work for Poor People*, Banque mondiale (Washington, DC: World Bank, 2004b).

6. M. Agarwal and D. Sengupta, 'Structural Adjustment in Latin America: Policies and Performance', *Economic and Political Weekly* 34, no, 44 (1999): 3129–36 (3129).

7. M. Nussbaum and A. Sen (eds), *The Quality of Life* (Oxford: Clarendon, 1993), 30–53; A. Sen, *Development as Freedom* (New York: Knopf, 1999).

8. A. C. Giovanni, R. Jolly and F. Stewart, *Adjustment with a Human Face: Protecting the Vulnerable and Promoting Growth. A Study by UNICEF*, 1st and 2nd edition (Oxford: Oxford University Press, 1987).

9. A. Fiszbein and N. R. Schady, *Conditional Cash Transfers: Reducing Present and Future Poverty*, World Bank Policy Report (Washington, DC: World Bank, 2009); J. E. Saavedra and S. Garcia, 'Impacts of Conditional Cash Transfer Programs on Educational Outcomes in Developing Countries: A Meta-Analysis', *RAND Working Paper*, 2012, 1–63.

At this time, social programmes, particularly in utility services such as gas and electricity, were seen as wasteful and a bottleneck to progress.[10] Corruption was a major headache for international donors as social programmes had been hampered by political patronage and weak governance. This made it difficult to track spending or effectively measure the impact of policies on beneficiaries. It also meant that wealthier groups could benefit from state subsidies intended for poorer segments of the population. This led to recommendations that countries implement targeting methods to identify and allocate subsidies directly to those most in need. As a result, policymakers insisted that governments provide their citizens with documentation to ensure they were more easily identifiable to international actors, the state and, increasingly, the financial sector.

Social protection was popular with left-leaning parties transitioning towards democratisation.[11] Poverty reduction schemes became synonymous with the promotion of democratic values and the protection of the income poor.[12] Countries who participated in these programmes, particularly those with a weak human rights record, were able to present a new image of modernisation and inclusion through the implementation of strategies that guaranteed universal access to a basic income and welfare. In sum, social policy became a helpful political tool for states to prove that they were complying with international human rights norms by supporting institutions in addressing structural poverty.

While the Caribbean lagged behind, Latin America was quickly emerging as the world leader in tackling under-registration with a specific focus on birth registrations. In 2000 (Cartagena, Colombia) and 2002 (Lima, Peru), two conferences entitled 'Todos Contamos' ('We All Count') aimed to increase the reach of social programmes to encompass excluded groups, including Afro-descended and Indigenous populations. Around the same time, the World Conference against Racism, Racial Discrimination, Xenophobia and Related Intolerance (WCAR) in Durban, South Africa, highlighted under-registration as a matter of international concern for traditionally marginalised groups. As development specialists started to address the right of income-poor populations to state protection, national governments began to develop their own social protection strategies to improve well-being and distribute welfare payments to the poorest in their populations. Concerned about ineffective

---

10. Ibid.
11. E. Huber and J. D. Stephens, *Democracy and the Left: Social Policy and Inequality in Latin America*, (Chicago: University of Chicago Press, 2012).
12. J. Pribble, *Welfare and Party Politics in Latin America* (New York: Cambridge University Press, 2013).

resource distribution around the allocation of public spending to the income-poor, the World Bank and the Inter-American Development Bank (IADB) looked at new ways to synchronise messaging around poverty reduction.[13] Legal identity therefore became an intrinsic component of policies that aimed to modernise and improve the efficiency of government administrations.[14]

Identifying and Targeting the Income-Poor: The Conditional Cash Transfer

The most popular and successful poverty reduction strategy to target income-poor populations is the conditional cash transfer (CCT). By the mid-2000s, Chile (*Chile Solidario, 2002*), Argentina (*Plan Família*, 2002), Peru (*Perú Juntos*, 2005) and the Dominican Republic (*Solidaridad*, 2005) had all developed and started implementing their own national registration strategies. These countries started extending their CCT programmes, and by 2008, CCTs had reached 22 million families and 100 million individuals. This accounted for almost one-fifth of the regional population.[15]

International development specialists have dubbed CCTs the 'magic bullet in development' due to their capacity to disburse cash payments directly to those most in need.[16] Identification is a 'major pillar' of this model,[17] which identifies and tracks populations eligible for state welfare. This is seen as a robust way to ensure that payments are distributed effectively by reaching targeted individuals.

13. R. Sánchez, 'Hacia un Plan Nacional de Documentación de Dominicanos(as): Diagnóstico, Objetivos, Lineamientos Estratégicos y Componentes, 2006, Serie Protección Social No. 3. Programa de Apoyo a la Reforma y Modernización del Poder Ejecutivo. Secretariado Técnico de la Presidencia, Santo Domingo.

14. For some examples of recent identification programmes promoted by international organisations, see the World Bank's Identification for Development (ID4D), the IADB's Civil Registration and Identity Management initiative and Plan International's Universal Birth Registration.

15. Economic Commission for Latin America and the Caribbean, *Time for Equality: Closing Gaps, Opening Trails* (Brasilia: Economic Commission for Latin America and the Caribbean, 2010), 181.

16. In 2004, Nancy Birdsall, president of the Center for Global Development, stated in an interview with the *New York Times*: 'I think these programs [CCTs] are as close as you can come to a magic bullet in development. [...] They're creating an incentive for families to invest in their own children's futures. Every decade or so, we see something that can really make a difference, and this is one of those things.'

17. S. Duryea, A. Olgiati and L. Stone, *The Under-Registration of Births in Latin America* (Washington, DC: Inter-American Development Bank, 2006), 13–14.

CCTs rely on the strong institutional capacity of the state as well as the involvement of a variety of stakeholders, including cooperation from the church, religious leaders, social workers, NGOs, teachers and healthcare professionals.[18] While the income-poor are the targets of CCTs, for enhanced efficiency the model facilitates the collation of data across populations from people of varying socioeconomic backgrounds. CCTs can also be used to encourage behavioural changes in beneficiaries who need to comply with agreed 'conditionalities' so that they can receive cash payments. Welfare can be halted if people do not meet these requirements.[19] Failure to comply, including a lack of state-approved documentation, can mean that beneficiaries are removed from welfare programmes altogether. Of course, a welfare beneficiary must be a citizen to be eligible for a cash transfer payment, and a lack of legal documentation would exclude an individual from inclusion onto a welfare programme.

Social Policy as a Strategy to Target Dominican Populations and Tackle Under-Registration

The first Dominican CCT programme *Solidaridad* was inspired by *Chile Solidario*. The model marked each beneficiary with their own unique number, which allowed state officials to select welfare recipients using the country's civil registry, the Central Electoral Board, JCE. *Solidaridad* became the 'main social policy instrument utilised by the Dominican state in its fight against poverty'.[20] The Dominican CCT programme was ambitious and unique to Latin America. It was the first country to involve a non-state banking partner, Visa International, to disburse cash transfer payments via an electronic welfare card. This novel idea was based on the poverty identification model Sisbén in Colombia, an electronic system that formed part of a public–private agreement with banks. *Solidaridad* therefore depended on a strong relationship with the private sector, including Dominican banks and businesses,[21] who had

---

18. Fiszbein and Schady, *Conditional Cash Transfers*, 100; T. Britto, *Recent Trends in the Development Agenda of Latin America: An Analysis of Conditional Cash Transfers* (Manchester: Institute for Development Policy and Management, 2005).

19. This can include the targeting of teenage mothers to encourage regular health visits or vaccination programmes for the elderly. The use of CCTs as a means to distribute the COVID-19 vaccine and monitor uptake would make a fascinating study, for example.

20. S. Martí i Puig, D. Sánchez-Ancochea and A. Stein, *Producción del documento de sistematización de la experiencia en la implementación de la estrategia Progresando con Solidaridad* (Salamanca: Fundación General de la Universidad de Salamanca, 2015), 5.

21. Local Dominican banks involved in the scheme included BanReservas, Asociación de Prestamos, Asociación Cibao and Asociación la Nacional de Ahorros y Préstamos.

committed to ensuring that the card would work correctly and that payments would be made on time. *Solidaridad* was ambitious in scale, reaching one-third of Dominican families with some form of subsidy payment.

In the mid-2000s, around one-fifth of Dominicans and 60 per cent of the income poor had no form of documentation whatsoever.[22] This significant number of undocumented people presented a stumbling block to the successful implementation of CCTs. To improve the reach of CCTs, and in alignment with ambitious aims to overhaul the Dominican social policy sector, the government introduced three new departments.[23] First, the Unified Beneficiary Identification System (SIUBEN) identified and selected the households eligible for state subsidy payments. Second, the Social Grants Administration Department (ADESS) administered and disbursed these payments. Third, the CCT initiative *Programa Solidaridad* monitored beneficiaries through door-to-door visits and provided compulsory training sessions for welfare recipients. The effective registration and documentation of beneficiaries was fundamental to the successful functioning of *Solidaridad*. As one former World Bank official told me:

> The only way you get to be a beneficiary of *Solidaridad* is as a Dominican. [...] If you don't have a birth certificate, you really don't have any legal existence.[24]

International donors saw the introduction of this new social policy architecture a positive change that represented a landmark shift towards greater transparency of the social assistance sector. It formed part of the National Strategy for Development 2030, which aimed to take Dominicans out of

---

22. F. Regalia and M. Robles, *Social Assistance, Poverty and Equity in the Dominican Republic, Economic and Sector Study Series* (Washington, DC: Inter-American Development Bank, 2005), 2; H. Carrasco, E. G. Sandro Parodi and M. Vásquez, *¿Cómo se redistribuyen los recursos públicos en República Dominicana?* (Washington, DC: Banco Interamericano de Desarrollo, 2016).

23. The Social Protection Program was established via Decree No. 1554-04 in 2004 to oversee the Social Cabinet. The decree determined that state subsidies and CCTs should use SIUBEN to target social programme beneficiaries. SIUBEN and ADESS were also established the same year via Decrees 1073-04 and 1560-04, respectively. Programa Solidaridad was created via Decree 536-05 on 20 September 2005.

24. I interviewed Samuel Carlson, principal economist and social inclusion, education and childhood development specialist who from 2004 until 2007 was responsible for the elaboration and implementation of the World Bank Social Protection Investment Project. This was a major initiative which financed the nationwide expansion of legal identity practices. This included improvements to the Dominican civil registry, communications and outreach programmes and large-scale registration drives.

structural poverty and facilitate their participation as social actors.[25] In 2003, Banco Intercontinental (BanInter), one of the largest local Dominican banks, collapsed. This sent the economy into freefall. Struggling to cope, the peso began to tank and rapidly depreciated by 173 per cent (from 17.6 pesos per dollar in January 2003 to 48.1 by June 2004).[26] The price of basic goods, including food, rose sharply. From the start of 2003 until May 2004, 1.4 million people (around 15 per cent of the population) had sunk into poverty and 600,000 people were living in extreme poverty (6.5 per cent).[27]

Consumers began to absorb the high costs of fuel, gas and electricity. A lack of oil caused widespread blackouts, leaving some neighbourhoods without power for extended periods and the government struggling to keep the lights on.[28] Long power cuts and rising fuel prices were met with social unrest and protests. External funders became deeply worried about these escalating levels of instability and poverty. Dominican social spending had reached one of its highest levels since 1995 (Lizardo, 2005, p. 18). Due to significant deficiencies and bottlenecks within the sector, wealth remained firmly concentrated within elite circles and economic prosperity failed to 'trickle down' to the majority poor. Rather than lead to a reduction in poverty, the country experienced 'trade-offs between economic and social policy'.[29]

The World Bank used the leverage it had over the country's failing electricity sector and the government's attempts to import oil to try and push through new policy reforms that prioritised legal identity. To confront rising economic instability, the World Bank agreed to quickly disburse funds to the government via an emergency $100 million Social Crisis Response Adjustment Loan (SCRAL).[30] The SCRAL placed conditions on the implementation of monetary legislation and a new social assistance strategy.[31] This included the issuance of 11,000 birth certificates, the selection of beneficiaries for a non-contributory health insurance programme, the elimination of a minimum of five ineffective

25. MEPyD, *La Ley Orgánica de la Estrategia Nacional de Desarrollo de la República Dominicana 2030 (END)* (Santo Domingo: MEPyD, 2012).
26. See World Bank, *Dominican Republic Social Protection Investment Loan. Report No: 36299-DO* (Santo Domingo: World Bank, 2007), 1.
27. Ibid.
28. E. Hayes de Kalaf, 'Electricidad y Equidad en la República Dominicana: Una Perspectiva del Desarrollo Humano' Santo Domingo, 2010, 11–12.
29. S. A. Johnson, 'State-Led Growth and Development', in *Challenges in Health and Development* (Berlin: Springer Science + Business Media, 2011), 71–101 (76).
30. World Bank, *Social Crisis Response Adjustment Loan (SCRAL) between Dominican Republic and International Bank for Reconstruction and Development, No.7215-DO* (Santo Domingo: World Bank, 2004a).
31. UNDP, *Política social II: capacidades y derechos. Análisis y propuestas de políticas sociales en República Dominicana* (Santo Domingo: UNDP, 2010), 201–21.

social programmes and the approval by the Ministry of Education of an operational manual for the cash transfer program.[32] This strategy relied on concrete steps to tackle levels of under-registration and ensure welfare payments were reaching the targeted – Dominican – populations.

The enthusiasm with which the Dominican government began to reach out to previously informal populations and collate their personal data marked a dramatic change in the country. Initially, the authorities had lacked the strong political will to address the under-registration of the Haitian-descended. The business sector had exploited informalities in the employment sector to avoid paying health insurance and investing in pensions. A strong nationalist faction within Congress also vehemently rejected criticism of its treatment of migrants and their children. The Unit of Social Information (UIS) began working with a technical team of lawyers and civil registry officials at the Social Cabinet to coordinate, plan and monitor the National Plan for the Provision of Identity Documents. The plan was part of measures to support the reform and modernization of the executive power and was the first national strategy to tackle under-registration across the country. National coverage of social policy under the Social Cabinet expanded rapidly. Vice president Rafael Alburquerque, a lawyer and highly respected defender of Dominican workers' rights, oversaw the running of all social assistance and protection programmes from 2004 to 2012.

I spoke with the former directors of SIUBEN, ADESS and the *Solidaridad* programme (2004–12) to learn more about the pivotal role they had played in helping expand legal identity measures: Miriam Rodríguez de Simó (SIUBEN), Van Elder Espinal Martínez (ADESS) and Fernando Reyes Castro (*Solidaridad*). As former director of SIUBEN, Rodríguez de Simó immediately acknowledged problems with the identification of Dominicans, noting:

> Health and education are both a matter of human rights and are within the Constitution. Dominicans have a right to these services. They should all have the same level of access. That was the vision of the targeting model. We have to revise what the targeting models are and ensure that any gaps are closed.

Rodríguez de Simó said she was proud of the strong database SIUBEN had developed particularly now that it could identify 'anomalies' within the system. She told me how social protection was for everyone; documented and undocumented (Dominican) populations, men and women alike. Those without their paperwork were encouraged to try and get their documents via

---

32. World Bank, *Social Crisis Response Adjustment Loan*, 14.

World Bank–sponsored communication campaigns and outreach programmes, which included the support of the church and local NGOs.[33] If an individual did not have their documentation, they were told to take someone in their household to help them register. Rodríguez de Simó saw this as a question of complete transparency and the only way to strengthen programme capacity. An individual could not get their cash transfer payment without being registered. It was a question of logic, she said.

She recounted how gradually Dominicans were starting to view access to welfare, health and education as a right. People now went to public offices to demand their documentation. They asked to be included onto welfare programmes. Through these practices, people were learning to claim specific services and articulate their demands to the state. She thought that this represented a huge cultural shift in a country with a strong history of clientelism:

> Before they [the state] used to give you things. You received them but there was no sense of responsibility. That vision has changed because there was a complete conceptual redesign of social policy, a new methodological approach. [...] People *reclama* [demand a service]. They go to a system and ask for their money now. Having a card has a value for them. They ask to be registered.

When I spoke with Van Elder Espinal Martínez, he proudly referred to ADESS as a 'Sisbén *aplatanado*' (a Dominicanised Sisbén). Inspired by the success of the Colombian model, he told me how the authorities had travelled extensively throughout the region, learning from experiences and sharing ideas. He had participated in roadshows with international banks, telling me of the crucial role private sector investment had played in helping develop this new social policy strategy. Once established, ADESS was channelling around 2 billion US dollars. It was a major and ambitious undertaking, he told me.

Espinal Martínez gave a detailed description of the economic crisis saying he saw this as a motivating factor in improving the targeted distribution of subsidy payments to Dominicans. He talked about the high levels of inflation, food prices and gas and electricity tariffs explaining that in the mid-2000s life had become very expensive for everyone. The way the government was distributing subsidy payments at that time was wasteful and no longer financially viable. He said that the system in place was very weak, and there was a need to

---

33. World Bank, *Project Appraisal Document on a Proposed Loan in the Amount of US$19.4 Million to the Dominican Republic for a Social Protection Investment Project. Dominican Republic Social Protection Investment Loan. Report No: 36299-DO* (Washington, DC: World Bank, 2007).

create a specialised agency that could administrate all of the social subsidies. The government needed to develop a more efficient, transparent system of payment that would generate credibility and ensure that subsidy payments were reaching the 'right' sectors of the population. This strategy hinged on the effective targeting and identification of 'suitable' beneficiaries.[34] He saw the magnitude and reach of these efforts as an enormous achievement, stating:

> [The social protection system] is one of the most important advances in the last 100 years. Almost 80% of Dominicans now have health insurance. Before, we didn't have the structure in place. Now we know how many poor people we have and where they are.

Espinal Martínez told me how the government had carried out a nation-wide 'sweep' across both deprived and wealthier neighbourhoods, in rural and urban areas, to collate household data from everyone. It was very big undertaking, reaching 90 per cent of the income-poor. By 2006, the state had already identified 600,000 families eligible for welfare. When it had finished, this number was close to one million. I asked Espinal Martínez if there had been any difficulties in the implementation of the social protection programme. While he did not specifically mention the experiences of Haitian-descended populations, he did state that the task of deciding which beneficiaries should be included in these programmes had been a particularly difficult process.

The ex-director of *Solidaridad*, Fernando Reyes Castro, told me that the last important step in social protection was the CCT programme because it reminded beneficiaries of their rights and responsibilities as citizens and included sanctions for non-compliance. The state saw the electronic payment card as a way to directly reach Dominicans and influence lasting behavioural changes. This included ensuring that parents would now get birth documentation for their children and register them in school. The rollout of this model included interventions at public clinics and hospitals and initiatives to monitor school attendance and promote vaccinations.

Women and mothers were an important focus of *Solidaridad* because they were seen as the vehicle through which the state could improve the health and well-being of their children. Cash payments were dependent upon the number of children in school and training sessions were targeted at mothers. The state encouraged women to give birth in public hospitals rather than at home to facilitate the registration of their children. According to Reyes Castro, approximately 70–80 per cent of persons declared as heads of household were women and typically the registration process took place via the woman.

---

34. He meant Dominicans.

Solidaridad representatives would collate personal data about a woman and her family, and this information would be sent to ADESS to arrange payments by linking the electronic card to the woman's details. The Secretary for Health became more involved too using the statistics collated to help reduce maternal death rates. Families received training on how to use the card. Beneficiaries were told they could no longer share or swap their ID with other people as they had perhaps done so in the past to help a friend or a neighbour visit the doctor or register their baby. There were commercial products tied to the card, including what beneficiaries were allowed purchase and where. Each beneficiary was told about the programme and the duties they were expected to fulfil.

Haitian-Descended Populations and Legal Identity: The Elephant in the Room

To gain a deeper understanding of how legal identity had become such a core focus of Dominican social policy, I spoke with four people who were instrumental to the conceptualisation and expansion of measures across the country: Samuel Carlson (former World Bank employee), Enrique Ogando (former director of the Legal Identity Documentation Component, Social Protection Investment Project, CDD-PIPS), Odalys Otero Núñez (director of the National School of Electoral Training and Civil Status, EFEC) and Brígida Sabino (director of the Inspections Department at the JCE). Carlson was a principal economist and social inclusion, education and childhood development specialist at the World Bank. From 2004 until 2007, he spearheaded the implementation of the World Bank Social Protection Investment Project. This was a major initiative that financed the nationwide expansion of legal identity. It included the provision of funding to the state to improve its civil registry and the implementation of outreach programmes and large-scale registration drives.

Carlson told me just how politically sensitive the issue of under-registration was on the island. He said that initially the government had lacked motivation in addressing the problem because of the high levels of informality and the political sensitivities associated with registrations. A large number of Dominicans had no form of documentation to verify their legal existence. This was a problem for the Haitian-descended. He said:

> No one had wanted to get involved in the identification issue on any large scale because it was so politically charged [...] it was the elephant in the room. [...] The Dominican government has never been particularly motivated to discuss the issue of documentation. This is given the

history between the Dominican Republic and Haiti when hundreds of thousands of Haitian workers were brought over during the Trujillo era to work in the sugar cane plantations. They were undocumented, they didn't have passports. They had children. The Dominican Republic never wanted to acknowledge the children of Haitians as Dominicans even though their law stated that if you were born in the country, you were Dominican.

Carlson directly linked the expansion of legal identity, as promulgated by the World Bank, with historical tensions that had been building on the island, particularly strategic efforts to address the 'Haitian' problem. He told me:

They [the authorities] didn't want to encourage more Haitians to come over to have their children there. They were afraid of the Haitian 'horde invasion'. It's a very powerful narrative. Politically, no one wanted to deal with these undocumented children. The World Bank was saying, 'Look if we're going to help you with social policy, if we're going to help you with the social protection plan [...] that's got to reach the most vulnerable Dominicans in your population.' The ones that were the most vulnerable, however, were the ones with no legal existence. So, the World Bank pushed for that to happen.

Our conversation highlighted the strong political component of civil registrations and the difficult relationship that had developed between the Social Cabinet and the World Bank. Carlson said that the technical coordinator at the Social Cabinet, Susana Gámez, was working in a very challenging environment. He told me there was a tension between her need to maintain the technical integrity of the project and balance this against external pressure from both international donors and Dominican political actors.

Carlson said that at some point during the mid-2000s, the World Bank had fallen out with the Dominican government and began to disagree over the content of its operational manual.[35] He said the government felt the World Bank was intervening too much in the project. After months of design work, the relationship between Gámez's political bosses and the World Bank technical bosses became very fraught. Opposition members of Congress wanted to make sure that the *Solidaridad* welfare cards would not be used to the political advantage of the ruling party, the Partido de la Liberación Dominicana

---

35. Programa Solidaridad, *Manual Operativo del Programa Solidaridad. Gabinete de Política Social* (Santo Domingo: Gabinete de Política Social, 2006).

(Dominican Liberation Party, PLD) or be perceived by the public as simply a cash handout to gain votes.

Notwithstanding, Dominican politicians understood the importance and the value of a legal identity. Members of the opposing party the Partido Revolucionario Dominicano (Dominican Revolutionary Party, PRD) welcomed the intervention of the World Bank because it could act as an external arbiter over registrations. As Carlson noted:

> Dominican politicians certainly understood the importance at a basic human level of helping people who didn't have documents get documents. People are *jodido* ('fucked') without their ID. They knew how hard and important it was to get one. [...] They wanted to have eyes on how the project was implemented so that it was fair. The World Bank involvement in the project was welcomed by Congress because they did not trust that the Executive Branch would carry this out in an objective, technical manner. They assumed it would be carried out in a political manner as had been [the case] historically.

Carlson said he was concerned that, due to a lack of birth certificates, children were being excluded from a primary education. He said the Dominican government was already 'ahead of the game' in trying to identify some of these populations for inclusion into the education sector. There were huge levels of informality, and Carlson was conscious that without legal identity documentation, thousands of children would be unable to enrol in school.[36] He noted how the then Secretary of Education (SEE) had already started to develop a database from school registrations with a list of names of children whose parents had tried but were unable to register them due to a lack of sufficient documentation. He told me that he went directly to the SEE to get a copy of this database. At that time, data was stored in a rudimentary manner on an old desktop computer in a tiny office. Enthusiastic about the opportunity this presented to improve technologies and the way in which the authorities were storing their data, Carlson began to work with the World Bank to set

---

36. In my interview with a Dominican high school director, the woman acknowledged that it was becoming more difficult to register children at her institution. She said, however, that this changing situation made little difference to her because, whether permitted or not, she would still strive to ensure that she registered all children at her school regardless of whether or not they had their ID. Although it was becoming much harder to formally enrol a child in school without a valid birth certificate, she saw a child's education as her priority. The director reasoned that the children at her school still had to sing the anthem every day and pledge allegiance to the Dominican flag. This, she told me, made it very clear to her where their loyalties lay, not the document they were asked to show her.

numerical targets to facilitate the recording of birth certificates for Dominican children to attend school. He said:

> These were tremendously vulnerable children and that's why going back to the quick disbursement adjustment loan there were conditionalities in there about the documentation of Dominican children. There were specific numerical targets about x number of thousands of Dominican children who needed to get their birth certificates in order to be registered in school.

Interventions to provide children with a birth certificate logically began taking place at public hospitals. Officials would encourage women to register their babies. Problems quickly emerged with these tactics, however, particularly for Haitian migrants and undocumented women. Those without an ID were unable to register their children or were told to record them as Haitians. As Carlson noted:

> The JCE [civil registry] had the birth certificates issued at the hospital. They met with those folks to ask when the mother gave birth if they could get these birth certificates issued straight away rather than retroactively. [...] They certainly intervened [in the case of] women. If [a woman] had [her] ID, they would issue her with an *acta* [birth certificate]. If she didn't have a ID, they wouldn't. It was [all carried out] through the woman.

My conversation with Carlson confirmed the important role the World Bank had played in expanding legal identity measures. Not only did it provide the financial assistance to the authorities as a means to encourage more robust structural adjustment reforms, it also acted as the mediator between politicians and technical specialists to oversee the distribution of documentation. The World Bank therefore was absolutely central to the expansion of legal identity and in pushing Dominican nationalists to agree to the uptake of legal identity as a means to register those citizens the authorities deemed eligible to receive their documentation. Carlson noted, that politicians had become overly enthusiastic about the far-reaching potential of ID systems. He told me:

> In the DR [...] the pendulum swung so far that it became nearly impossible to get your [legal identity] documents if your parents did not have a *cédula*.

Next, I spoke with Enrique Ogando, the former director responsible for the legal identity component of the World Bank loan. Our conversation was brief as he was hesitant to talk with me in any great detail. Rather than focus on the impact of legal identity measures on people, he told me about the benefits of these changes for the private sector and the formal economy. Ogando noted the enthusiasm and support the programme had received from banks regarding efforts to formalise registration procedures which he considered both innovative and exciting. It was not simply an isolated initiative but one which required lasting support across all government ministries, institutions and banks. Everything was moving towards more effective targeting, he said. These improvements helped the state identify which beneficiaries were being included for state assistance and who was being left out. As he told me:

> You can't give resources to a person who does not meet the basic requirements […] to whom it [documentation] does not correspond. This makes things more transparent.

My conversation with Odalys Otero Núñez, a Cuban-Dominican and director of the EFEC, was enlightening particularly as she, like myself, had arrived in the country as a foreign national and subsequently naturalised as a Dominican. A Cuban by birth, Otero Núñez had little sympathy for people who did not have their papers. She said that she had gone through the naturalisation process and did not see why others could not manage to do the same. Whereas other informants had mentioned a need to identify anomalies and close gaps within the system, Otero Núñez was the only government representative to explicitly mention concerns about Haitian migrants and their descendants born in the country and connect these with the expansion of recent social policy measures. She said that decades of Haitian immigration had created difficulties on the ground. Children born to Haitians, she argued, had increased social demands with regard to access to education and healthcare services. I asked what link existed between measures to document Dominicans and Haitian immigration into the country. She responded:

> In the Constitution, the children of foreigners are not Dominicans.[37] Haiti doesn't want to recognise their nationality either. Legally, they don't want to give them their documents. Some people say this is a form

---

37. This is a key argument of Dominican nationalists to justify why Haitian-descended populations have no claim to Dominican citizenship. This is only the case after administrative changes were introduced in 2007 and constitutional amendments were made in 2010. As we will see in Chapter 4, the Dominican civil registry (JCE) began

of statelessness. But it isn't. They aren't Dominicans. This gets mixed up. On the other hand, there are Dominicans and the children of Dominicans without documents of any kind. There is a problem. Even how to do the communications campaign to reach them.

Otero Núñez was critical of recent changes, saying that things had become far too rigid and there was no flexibility anymore. She lamented that sometimes the overhaul of the sector was causing more problems than it was solving, particularly for Dominicans who already held an older paper form of ID. She said the country had more pressing issues it needed to worry about. Many poor Dominicans lacked access to drinking water. There were not enough hospitals. Healthcare was inadequate and illiteracy widespread. While acknowledging improvements across government services, she argued that doctors still tended to patients – migrants and Dominicans alike – even if they were unable to produce a valid ID. In contrast to concerns expressed by international actors over the need to provide everyone with an ID, she thought that a lack of documentation did not necessarily block access to Haitians, Dominicans or anyone else who could not produce their paperwork. Unaware of global aims to achieve universal legal identity, she queried:

So, why all this effort now? Why even bother?

Finally, I went to the Dominican civil registry (JCE), an institution with strong political connections to the ruling PLD. Researchers and NGO representatives have rarely engaged with the civil registry when carrying out research on the impact of registrations on children born to Haitians. Nor have they approached state actors to talk about their role in citizenship-stripping practices. I was extremely thankful therefore that I could have such an open and frank discussion with Brígida Sabino, the director of the JCE Inspections Department. This was an important post as Sabino oversaw the team of lawyers responsible for inspecting and flagging up files containing potential 'anomalies'. This included persons of Haitian ancestry whose lived experiences we will continue to hear about in the upcoming chapters.

Sabino began working as a registry official in the eastern town of San Pedro de Macorís, the site where many of the first complaints arose over access to documentation. The town was one of the largest sugar-producing regions in the country and home to a high number of Haitian-descended and Black *cocolo* populations. When I arrived to meet with Sabino, I was immediately struck by the absence of *buscones* hanging around outside the

---

retroactively enforcing this logic, telling persons born between 1929 and 2007 that they should never have been granted Dominican citizenship.

building.[38] These were people who, until very recently, had maintained a permanent presence at government institutions. I was used to them calling out to me, trying to get a few hundred pesos in exchange for assistance in acquiring or legalising paperwork. Sabino spoke with pride about their disappearance, which she linked to changes that have modernised and digitised the civil registry. People no longer needed to pay the *buscones* as they could now resolve their own issues rather than taking the 'back door' approach, she told me.

To gain entry to Sabino's office, I had to walk through a large warehouse containing discarded folders, office equipment and old computers stacked high up to the ceiling. Such chaotic scenes epitomised why Dominicans had dubbed the civil registry *el tollo* ('the mess') and had complained extensively about its inefficiency. Once I arrived at the Inspections Department, I could visibly see the dramatic changes that had taken place. I walked into the newly refurbished building where there was a comfortable air-conditioned office with row upon row of people working at their new computers. I learnt they were paralegals and law students assigned to scrutinise people's individual cases.

Sabino told me that her department worked in close collaboration with the Social Policy Cabinet, which was supported by World Bank funding. Their initial efforts, she noted, helped the state introduce new biometric technologies which were facilitating future registration procedures. Now they were able to share information across government ministries to verify mistakes and resolve problems that some people had been experiencing for years. Sabino eagerly told me what a transformative impact these policies were having on previously undocumented Dominicans:

> We tried to ensure that no one felt excluded. [...] When someone has spent their life as part of a social group that lives among themselves. [...] They breathe but they don't exist. When you give them their documentation you can see how people's faces change. The tiredness, all the work they had to go through. All of it was worth it. When you see the reaction of a mother when you give her a *cédula* and seven birth certificates to her children. Their smiles tell you that you have just changed someone's life.

Sabino echoed the discourse of international organisations and NGOs about the importance and the value an ID can hold for the individual. She was sure that documentation could help bolster a sense of common identity,

---

38. *Buscones* are tricksters who try and obtain money in exchange for documentation. People would pay *buscones* for help in obtaining paperwork. The authorities often saw them as a nuisance, and they had all but disappeared with the introduction of new technologies to facilitate registrations.

helping people feel proud to be a Dominican. This, she believed, gave people dignity and a sense of belonging. She stated this resulted in the increased agency and empowerment of individuals to demand their rights and claim services from the state. Sabino noted that there had been a cultural shift in the country which once had a tradition of gift-giving (known in Spanish as *el dao* or *la fundita*) in exchange for support for the regime.[39] Because ID practices were aimed specifically at mothers as the heads of households, she said it was women who had benefitted most from these changes:

> A woman with an ID can go out and earn a wage. She can open a beauty salon, have a bank account and get a mobile phone. A woman can ensure the home is connected to the electricity grid without resorting to the help of a family member or neighbour. She can also receive additional benefits, such as the school bonus, when she sends her children to school. Women therefore can *feel* the benefit of changes to the system.

Sabino linked the expansion of registrations on the island with a broader push to ensure that Dominican transnational populations were more easily identifiable. While failing to mention the overwhelmingly negative impact the decisions at her department were having on Haitian-descended populations, she instead spoke with real compassion about the experiences of undocumented Dominicans in the United States who, she noted, had 'fallen into illegality'. Sabino praised the introduction of measures that were now allowing this group to secure their documents without having to travel back to Santo Domingo.

There were clear political motivations for ensuring that Dominicans living abroad had access to an ID. Sabino told me how the new registrations were facilitating overseas voting, particularly for hundreds of thousands of Dominicans now living in New York. She recounted how the Dominican Consulate, located in Times Square, regularly issued up to eight hundred ID cards every day, sometimes more. This, she told me, has helped Dominicans get documents not only for themselves but also for their US-born children.

My conversation with Sabino highlighted how Dominican descendants living abroad – some of whom had never even set foot on the island – could now obtain their documentation more easily. At the same time, Dominican-born persons of Haitian ancestry, the majority of whom had never left the

---

39. The culture of gift-giving helped the state reinforce the cultural perception that public services, particularly utilities, were a gift from the president and therefore a social good. See UNDP, *Política social II: capacidades y derechos. Análisis y propuestas de políticas sociales en República Dominicana* (Santo Domingo: UNDP, 2010), 202.

Dominican Republic or ever been to Haiti, were struggling to get their legal identity papers and told they were Haitians. This, I felt, was a highly unjust and tremendously perverse situation.

In this chapter, I have highlighted the profound socioeconomic and social programme reforms that have taken place in Latin America and the Caribbean over the past three decades. These changes resulted in the introduction of new social protection mechanisms that have bolstered systems that identify and target poor populations for state subsidy payments. This has included the widespread promotion of the popular conditional cash transfer model, which has facilitated the registration of previously informal and/or undocumented populations for welfare assistance and inclusion into the financial sector.

In the case of the Dominican Republic, we have seen how, since the economic crash of the early 2000s, the state began to take advantage of social protection mechanisms to introduce targeted spending strategies which depended on improving the registration of the income-poor. International actors, such as the World Bank, the IADB and the United Nations, financed and facilitated the introduction of these mechanisms to target and strengthen the provision of legal identity documentation.

In the past, the elite had benefitted economically and politically from the under-registration of migrants, their descendants and income-poor Dominicans as they could exploit their labour by ignoring their requests for formal recognition and strategically distribute ID as a means to secure votes during elections. They were resistant to modernising the country's weak civil registry yet, in a complete U-turn, began to take advantage of increased investment in its social policy sector. This included the introduction of a 'tripod' of the state institutions SIUBEN, ADESS and *Solidaridad*, which administered and disbursed welfare payments to Dominicans. Through these institutions, and with the support of external donors and the banking sector, the state began to collate and administer data across the education, health and social assistance sectors. It introduced more sophisticated technologies and invested money in the civil registry so that it could identify individual files within the system. This allowed the state not only to better identify Dominicans it deemed eligible for state subsidies but also to bolster state architectures to allow them to retroactively and arbitrarily block the Haitian-descended from accessing their legal identity documentation. As we will see in the next chapter, non-governmental organisations (NGOs) began to denounce that children born to migrants were losing their nationality and were therefore being made stateless due to the refusal of some civil registry officials to issue them with a Dominican birth certificate. These disputes over access to documentation resulted in an intense battle between migrant rights NGOs and the state over who should have access to a Dominican legal identity.

Chapter 4

CITIZENS MADE FOREIGN: THE BATTLE FOR A DOMINICAN LEGAL IDENTITY

> By interpreting the application of the Constitution retroactively [the JCE] will have to tell people born in the country for up to eighty years that they are no longer Dominicans.[1]

In this chapter, we will explore the timeline of events in the build-up to the 2013 *Sentencia* that retroactively stripped the plaintiff Juliana Deguis Pierre of her Dominican nationality (Figure 3).[2] The ruling led to the implementation of a nationwide audit to identify tens of thousands of other foreign-descended people born since 1929[3] whose legal identity was now in dispute. We will examine the tug of war that took place between the Dominican state and migrant rights organisations who had mobilised in an effort to combat statelessness. As these campaigns gained traction, Dominican and international NGOs joined forces to demand the restitution of rights to affected populations, turning to the Inter-American system for support. In response, the authorities introduced stricter administrative barriers, ordering that civil registry officials challenge and investigate individuals they believed to be of Haitian descent. From the mid-2000s, the authorities introduced new legal, institutional, procedural, constitutional and administrative reforms which aimed to block persons of Haitian ancestry from acquiring evidentiary proof of their national status. Through a radical overhaul of the Dominican civil registry (Central

---

1. Original quote from Dominican journalist and activist Juan Bolívar Díaz: 'Tendrán que decirle que ya no son dominicanos a personas hasta de 80 años que nacieron en el país, en una aplicación retroactiva de una nueva interpretación de la Constitución.' Juan Bolívar Díaz, 'El Constitucional ignora la Corte Interamericana', *Hoy Periodico*, 2013.
2. See Sentencia TC/0168/13, *Referencia: Expediente número TC-05-2012-0077*. Santo Domingo, 2013.
3. The date the Dominican-Haitian border was formally established and the Dominican government first introduced the 'in transit' exception into its constitution.

Figure 3 'The Dominican Republic is my country': Protesting the 2013 *Sentencia*.
Credits: Lorena Espinoza Peña.

Electoral Board, JCE), the government developed a new legal definition of
the Dominican nationality that ultimately removed birthright citizenship from
Haitian-descended people with a view to blocking them from the body
politic altogether. This chapter concludes by examining some of the reactions
of NGOs and affected individuals who once thought they were citizens yet
were later informed they should never have been recognised as Dominicans
in the first place.

The Inter-American System, NGOs and the Fight against Statelessness

During a heated election campaign in 1996, the Dominican Liberation
Party (PLD) aligned with the xenophobic and ferociously anti-Haitian
National Progressive Force (FNP). Together they opposed the election of
José Francisco Peña Gómez, a Black man born to Haitian parents. This
political gamble may have secured Leonel Fernández the presidency (1996–
2000, 2004–8, 2008–12), but he was heavily criticised in international circles
for his close ties to the FNP. Bilingual Fernández, who grew up in New York,
positioned himself as a modern leader eager to distance the country from its

dictatorial past by embracing neoliberal reforms, economic expansion and technological advances.[4]

The president needed to prove to investors and international donors that the country was now a modern, global and democratic state that could remain politically and economically stable. While forced to appease the extreme nationalist factions within his own party, including the business elite who for decades had profited from the cheap labour provided by undocumented migrants, Fernández had to distance himself from the image of the leader of an anti-Haitian and fragile nation. To achieve this, he would have to improve engagement with international actors by demonstrating a greater acceptance of the human rights framework.

The mid-1990s marked a boom period for the Dominican Republic. Embracing neoliberal reforms and foreign multimillion-dollar investment, the country became the fastest growing economy in Latin America. Although the economy was thriving, traditional sectors, such as the sugar industry, were in rapid decline. With new investment in areas such as tourism, free trade zones and construction, Haitian-descended populations began moving away from the rural *batey* (sugar cane plantation). As they entered the formal economy, their presence within Dominican urban spaces was becoming more visible and their demands for formal documentation more vocal.

Human rights groups and NGOs campaigning for the rights of persons born to Haitian migrants to a Dominican birth certificate denounced that children were being rendered stateless due to their undocumented status.[5] Using a rights-based framework, activists and legal campaigners argued that Dominican children were being left without a nationality as state officials were refusing to issue them their Dominican birth certificate. Campaigners saw the practices of civil registry officials as a form of racial profiling against individuals who 'look[ed] Haitian'.[6] They demanded the state ensure their Dominican citizenship be formally recognised through the issuance of legal identity papers. These campaigns were reputationally

---

4. Among the numerous vanity projects that president Fernández entertained was the Caribbean's first ever Metro. Wishing to accomplish his dream of converting the Dominican capital city Santo Domingo into his very own 'New York Chiquito' (a tiny New York), and at a cost of hundreds of millions of dollars, Fernández built a subway in a country with one of the most fragile electricity sectors in the world and where most Dominicans experienced daily blackouts.

5. For a comprehensive overview of this story, see the work of J. Lyon, 'Inheriting Illegality: Race, Statelessness, and Dominico-Haitian Activism in the Dominican Republic', doctoral thesis, Florida International University, 2018.

6. Human Rights Watch, *We Are Dominican. Arbitrary Deprivation of Nationality in the Dominican Republic: Summary* (New York: Human Rights Watch, 2015), 15.

damaging to the government as it tried to improve its human rights image with regards to its treatment of Haitian migrants.

One important example of how campaigners harnessed regional support to fight the Dominican state is the case of Dilcia Oliven Yean and Violeta Bosico Cofi, two young girls whose mothers had tried unsuccessfully to register them using their own Dominican ID cards.[7] Civil registry officials informed the women that their children were 'in transit' and therefore ineligible for Dominican citizenship. In 1995, a lawyer and legal advisor to the Movement of Dominican-Haitian Women (MUDHA) intervened in the case and that of 18 other children from Sábana Grande de Boyá, a municipality in the Monte Plata province. Taking advantage of a newly introduced appeals process a few years later, lawyers were then able to contest these actions on the grounds of unconstitutionality. In September 2005, the Inter-American Court of Human Rights (IACHR) ruled the Dominican government had ignored constitutional guarantees with regard to the automatic acquisition of nationality and could not define the status of the girls born in the country as transitory, stating:

> [It is] unacceptable to describe the alleged victims [Dilcia and Violeta] as 'foreigners in transit' since those who live for 10, 15 or more years in a country cannot be described as transients.[8]

The court ruled that the concept of 'in transit' could not be equated with an irregular status, arguing that the Dominican state's refusal to provide the girls with a birth certificate as evidence of their juridical existence had kept them in a 'legal limbo', leaving them stateless and at risk of imminent expulsion to Haiti.

In an attempt to avoid further embarrassment about the incident and hoping to defuse condemnation about their actions, the civil registry backtracked and instead issued the two girls their Dominican birth certificates.[9] The court nevertheless insisted that the case continue. It urged the state to provide the girls with an apology and compensation and criticised the government's refusal

---

7. The court stated, for example, that the mother of Dilcia Yean had already registered one of her daughters, Magdalena, in October 2004. She was asked to present her Dominican *cédula*, witnesses and documentation from the church and the mayor. See IAHCR, *Case of the Girls Yean and Bosico v. Dominican Republic. Judgment of September 8, 2005*, 2005, 23.
8. Ibid.
9. To quell criticism of these practices, on 1 October 2001 the state informed the commission 'it ha[d] decided to grant birth certificates to the children,' noting that it had already issued the two girls with their documentation on 25 September 2001. Ibid., 6.

to register the children. It ruled that a lack of birth certificate had impeded their right to a free primary education, preventing them from exercising their full citizenship rights based on their ethnic origin.

The Dominican state, the IACHR maintained, had violated several articles within the Inter-American Convention on Human Rights. These included the right to a name and nationality, the right to recognition as a person before the law, the right to protection measures as children and the right to equal treatment before the law.[10] It ordered the government to establish a clear and fair appeals system, underlining the need to protect the human rights of vulnerable children of Haitian descent.

The decision set a precedent in the Americas as it was the first time a regional court had ruled on the sovereign issue of nationality provision. International actors, NGOs and state officials saw the rule of law and the integration of human rights norms as an important and necessary step to overcome statelessness. They supported the IACHR's view that the Dominican government had ignored constitutional guarantees on the automatic acquisition of nationality. They also agreed that a child could not retroactively inherit the migratory status of their parents, even when that status was illegal or not recognised.

Although the case centred on the right of the children to a state-issued Dominican birth certificate, less attention was paid to the mothers of the two girls. Both women had tried, albeit unsuccessfully, to register their daughters using their own Dominican national identity cards (Martínez, 2014, pp. 152–53). Through a focus on the vulnerability and the rights of the children, the ruling made limited mention of the problems documented adult populations were also facing in having their legal identity recognised. This is an important observation because, in parallel to these actions, the Dominican state was subtly introducing a series of administrative and procedural changes that not only blocked the Haitian-descended from acquiring their birth certificates but also stopped them from obtaining or renewing any new forms of documentation, including national identity cards and passports. While the international focus remained on the rights of children born to Haitian migrants to a Dominican birth certificate, in the background the state was introducing a myriad of complex measures aimed at blocking foreign-descended adults from their paperwork altogether.

One person directly impacted by these measures was Sonia Pierre, co-founder of MUDHA. Pierre was a documented woman of Haitian ancestry and a prominent advocate of the right of Haitian-descended populations to a Dominican nationality.[11] She became a hate figure for nationalists who

---

10. Ibid., 56.
11. Although they share the same name, Sonia Pierre was not related to the 2013 *Sentencia* plaintiff Juliana Deguis Pierre. In 2007, she was awarded the Robert F. Kennedy

saw her alignment with international NGOs as a betrayal to Dominicans. The presence of NGOs can be unwelcome in the country because some Dominicans believe there is an international plan to fuse Haiti and the Dominican Republic together as one island.[12] This is largely based on fears of a renewed 'invasion' when Haitians took over the island in a 22-year occupation following the Haitian Revolution. Nationalists exploit this fear by claiming that outsider interference into the 'Haitian' question presents a real and credible threat to the sovereignty of the Dominican people.[13] They see outsider interest in nationality issues as part of a broader, externally funded plot to attack the country.

As ludicrous as these claims may sound, the nationalist threat to annul the paperwork of Haitian-descended populations was very real. Following a request by Pelegrin Castillo of the ultranationalist FNP, Pierre was told that the civil registry had already taken the decision to revoke her Dominican birth certificate and she would therefore be rendered stateless.[14] When a Dominican journalist broke this story, the media used the opportunity to attack Pierre and further discredit the authenticity of her Dominican identity, decrying that she could never be a *dominicana neta* (a 'real' Dominican) due to her Haitian roots. Although eventually Pierre retained her Dominican documentation, the authorities knew they could weaponise fears around citizenship-stripping practices as a way to try to silence critics such as Pierre and create a climate of fear in the country.

Rectifying Administrative 'Oversights': General Migration Law 285-04 and the Registry of Foreigners

Just three months after the IACHR decision on 14 December 2005, the state won its Supreme Court ruling challenging the constitutionality of the General Migration Law.[15] The domestic court upheld the authorities' application of

---

Memorial Human Rights Award for her human rights activism. She died in 2011 at the age of 48.

12. US Government Cable, *Dominicans Angered by Verdict at Inter-American Court of Human Rights* (Santo Domingo: US Government Cable, 2005).

13. These arguments are even present among the Dominican diaspora. It is a tactic regularly used to discredit public figures who support Haitian migrants or Haitian interests. See, for example, R. Mercedes, *Denuncian intensiones en EEUU de fusionar RD con Haití, CDN Digital,* 2018, https://www.cdn.com.do/2018/08/14/denuncian-intensiones-eeuu-fusionar-rd-haiti.

14. US Government Cable, *Update on Maneuvers against Sonia Pierre, Haitian-Dominican Advocate* (Santo Domingo: US Government Cable, 2007).

15. The case was brought by the Jesuit Service for Refugees and Migrants (*Servicio Jesuita a Refugiados y Migrantes,* SJRM).

the 'in transit' status in the case of children born to undocumented parents arguing that children born to 'Haitians' were not Dominican nationals. In a victory to the nationalists, the court ruled that even if an individual could produce their birth certificate or ID card, the state could now refuse to recognise the validity of these documents.[16] Dominican lawmakers used this domestic ruling to justify the actions of registry officials who had been refusing to issue birth certificates to persons born to Haitian parents, arguing that the possession of a state-issued birth certificate did not automatically entitle a person to a Dominican nationality.[17] In addition, the authorities claimed that they were rectifying an administrative oversight that had led to the erroneous inclusion of persons born to undocumented migrants within the civil registry since 1929. Using this logic, they not only restricted access to Dominican documentation to children born after 2004 but also began blocking persons born before this date from (re)obtaining their papers. It subsequently became much harder for anyone born to migrants to apply for or renew Dominican paperwork.

As problems over the identification of Dominican citizens continued, staff working on the expansion of legal identity measures at the Inter-American Development Bank (IADB) raised their concerns. One report acknowledged the difficulties in ascertaining the 'legitimacy' of many citizens, stating:

> While we cannot distinguish between children of native-born versus foreign-born, we recognize that the large presence and low status of Haitian migrants in the Dominican Republic may be driving this result.[18]

Other international donors, such as the World Bank, were reluctant to publicly challenge or criticise the actions of the state. They argued that disputes over access to citizenship should remain a sovereign matter enforceable

---

16. In 2014, the IACHR brought its judgement against the Dominican state in the *Case of Expelled Dominicans and Haitians v. Dominican Republic*. It used the ruling as an opportunity to further criticise measures implemented after the 2013 Constitutional Tribunal ruling. It noted: 'By considering said persons were aliens and requiring them to undertake a procedure to accede to the nationality that corresponded to them as of their birth, Law No. 169 represented an impediment to the full exercise of the right to nationality of the victims.' See Inter-American Court of Human Rights, *Case of Expelled Dominicans and Haitians v. Dominican Republic*, 2014.

17. J. M. Castillo Pantaleón, *La Nacionalidad Dominicana* (Santo Domingo: Editora Nacional, 2012).

18. S. Duryea, A. Olgiati and L. Stone, *The Under-Registration of Births in Latin America* (Washington, DC: Inter-American Development Bank, 2006), 9.

through domestic laws.[19] Rather than address what officials saw as the 'Haitian problem', the World Bank instead focused its money and resources on improving the targeting and identification of income-poor Dominicans. They gave technical assistance to the state to roll out large-scale registrations which provided the individuals they identified as Dominicans with a legal identity. It also funded a communications campaign that emphasised the importance of Dominican citizenship laws in the country.[20]

In parallel to this social assistance, the government began introducing changes to its legal framework with the intention of further stopping the Haitian-descended from accessing their papers. The first major overhaul of Dominican migration law since the 1930s took place in 2004 with the introduction of the General Law on Migration 285-04.[21] The law conflicted with the existing *jus soli* provision within the Dominican Constitution that recognised (most) Dominican-born children as nationals.[22] It also introduced important changes to visa categories for migrants and temporary visitors and took measures to improve regularisations for foreign nationals.

President Hipólito Mejía approved the law at 11 p.m. on 15th August 2004, the final day of his outgoing PRD (Partido Revolucionario Dominicano) and the last major piece of legislation the party passed.[23] After four years away from

---

19. World Bank, *Project Appraisal Document on a Proposed Loan in the Amount of US$19.4 Million to the Dominican Republic for a Social Protection Investment Project. Dominican Republic Social Protection Investment Loan. Report No: 36299-DO* (Washington, DC: World Bank, 2007), 17. *Political/social risk*: Addressing the exclusion of undocumented families is a very sensitive topic in Dominican society, linked to fears of Haitian immigration on one side and accusations that the Dominican Government applies discriminatory policies against Haitians on the other side. Both aspects of this risk need to be addressed. The 'nationalist' aspect would be minimised through consultations with Congress, meetings held with all political groups, respect for national laws regarding citizenship and promotion of public debate through church groups and prominent civil society organizations. The Catholic Church, in particular, has been vocal and proactive in supporting undocumented families and has supported efforts to simplify documentation processes. In addition, since July 2005 all major newspapers have regularly reported on this issue of undocumented Dominicans, which has served to increase public understanding of the issue, making the public less susceptible to extreme nationalist rhetoric.
20. See World Bank, 'Sub-Component 1', 8–9.
21. See Gobierno Dominicano, *Reglamento de migración n° 279, del 12 de mayo de 1939*, Santo Domingo, 1939.
22. Asamblea Nacional, *Constitución de la República Dominicana de 2010*, 2010.
23. For a background into the tensions over how this law was debated, see Lozano, Wilfredo. 2008. *La paradoja de las migraciones: El Estado Dominicano frente a la inmigración Haitiana*. Editorial UNIBE, FLACSO, SJRM. Santo Domingo: Editor Búho.

office, the PLD government, led by former president Leonel Fernández, returned to power in 2004.[24] International donors welcomed the return of Fernández, who worked closely with the World Bank to fund the country's social assistance strategy.[25] The new Fernández-led PLD administration used this legislation to start expanding its concept of 'in transit'. The term classified any person without a government-issued residency permit as a non-resident.[26] It further defined non-residents as temporary labourers and seasonal workers, such as persons working on sugar plantations and cross-border dwellers, and included migrants working in accordance with assigned quotas, such as political migration plans which secured temporary low-paid labour directly from Haiti. This non-resident category also applied to tourists, visa over-stayers and undocumented migrants.

In addition to these new classifications, Law 285-04 established the creation of a Registry of Foreigners. This new registry allowed officials to move persons once recorded within the civil registry as Dominican citizens and reclassify them as foreign nationals. Although not immediately put into practice,[27] the registry ensured that persons born on or after 16 August 2004 deemed to be 'in transit' and would instead be classed as foreigners.

The US embassy, aware of the potential negative consequences of these measures on persons whose state membership was in dispute, nevertheless supported the introduction of this new registry, stating:

The lack of documentation is an ongoing issue in the country. The JCE [civil registry] estimates as many as six hundred thousand Dominicans do not have birth certificates and [sic] as many as two hundred thousand do not have cedula [sic]. A number of these individuals are ostensibly

---

24. From 2000 to 2004, opposition leader Hipólito Mejía was president of the Dominican Revolutionary Party (Partido Revolucionario Dominicano, PRD). He was an extremely divisive figure and widely blamed for plummeting the country into a deep economic recession. International organisations, such as the World Bank, saw Fernández as a much safer and reliable candidate for the presidency.

25. UNDP, *Política social II: capacidades y derechos. Análisis y propuestas de políticas sociales en República Dominicana* (Santo Domingo: UNDP, 2010), 202.

26. The 2004 General Law on Migration 285-04 defined a person without the legitimate legal right of abode as a non-resident and anyone without a government-issued residency permit a 'foreigner in transit'. Sección VII: '4 De los no residentes Art.36: son admitidos como no residentes los extranjeros que califiquen en algunas de las siguientes subcategorías: 10. los no residentes son considerados personas en tránsito, para los fines de la aplicación del Artículo 11 de la Constitución de la República.' See Congreso Nacional de la República Dominicana, *Ley 285 sobre migración* (Santo Domingo: Gobierno Dominicano, 2004).

27. The Registry of Foreigners began on 18 April 2007 and was fully implemented in 2014, after the *Sentencia* decision which ordered the roll out of large-scale registration drives.

Dominicans of Haitian descent, many of who [*sic*] insist on Dominican nationality as opposed to bing [*sic*] registered as a foreigner. While the governmnt [*sic*] deserves credit for implementing the Registry o [*sic*] Foreigners, much more needs to be done to effectively address the issue of documenting individuas [*sic*] who are presently functionally stateless.[28]

In alignment with these new measures that bureaucratically reclassified Dominicans as foreign migrants, in 2007 the civil registry implemented increasingly arbitrary practices through the introduction of Resolution 012-07. This resolution allowed civil registry officials to refuse birth certificates to the children of foreigners whose status they suspected to be illegal.[29] It instructed registry officials to 'meticulously examine' documentation when reissuing copies of birth certificates[30] to allow state officials to challenge the validity of a person's citizenship status not solely at the point of birth registration – in the case of late registrations for undocumented adults – but also if the applicant needed to renew or obtain a copy of their identity card.

As a result, registry officials asked that migrant parents prove the legality of their residency status to obtain birth documentation for their children. Initially, persons who could not prove they were born to Dominican parents before 1950 would be allowed to naturalise as citizens, those born between 1951 and 1990 would be given permanent residency as foreigners and those born between 1991 and 14 August 2004 would be given temporary residency.[31] These conditions applied to all persons born to foreign parents (or parents a civil registry official suspected of not being Dominican) and were not exclusive to Haitian-descended populations. If a civil registry official identified an irregularity, he or she was ordered not to issue, sign or copy documentation and to report the file to the administrative department. This included the identification of persons whose parents had recorded their birth yet did so without using a state-issued identity card. State officials then began to apply this logic retroactively, refusing to record births or issue documentation to persons born to non-Dominican parents.

There were clear strategies to target women using these practices. The civil registry ordered public maternity clinics issue one of two hospital birth records known as a *Constancia de Nacido Vivo* (Riveros, 2014, pp. 66–67). The two forms

28. US Government Cable, *Open Society Justice Initiative Condemns DR Birth Registration System* (Santo Domingo: US Government Cable, 2008b).

29. Civil registry officials used a number of justifications for not issuing documents. These included a foreign-sounding surname or assuming an individual's parents were not Dominicans. We explore some of these examples in greater depth in Chapter 5.

30. See K. Civolani Hischnjakow, *Vidas Suspendidas: Efectos de la Resolución 012-07 en la población* (Santo Domingo: Centro Bonó, 2011), 69–86.

31. US Government Cable, 'Government Announces Documentation Initiative', *Revista Estudios Sociales* 41, no. 154 (2009b).

made the distinction between Dominican and foreign children. Babies thought to be born to Dominican mothers received a white slip and those thought to be born to foreign mothers received a pink slip. These new administrative procedures had a significant impact on documented and undocumented Haitian-descended mothers as well as Haitian women with Dominican partners who found it increasingly difficult to register their children.[32] Because this practice was largely carried out through the mother, it effectively bypassed the involvement of the father, who, even if in possession of a valid Dominican ID card, was excluded from registering a birth (Petrozziello et al., 2014). A child categorised by civil registry officials as a non-national was then recorded within the Registry of Foreigners alongside their mother.

The 2010 Dominican Constitution, the Constitutional Tribunal *Sentencia* 168-13 and the National Regularisation Plan 169-14

For over eighty years, the Dominican Constitution recognised the right of 'all people born on Dominican territory' to *jus soli* (birthright) citizenship (Figure 4). The two exceptions to this rule were children born to diplomats and persons 'in transit'. From 2008, the PLD began proposing highly controversial, ultra-Conservative changes to the constitution, angering environmental, women's and LGBTQ+ rights campaigners with sweeping reforms that ultimately extended the re-election term, prioritised private property rights, outlawed abortion under all circumstances and explicitly recognised marriage as a single union between a man and a woman.

Promulgated on 26 January 2010 – a mere two weeks after the devastating earthquake that had killed over 200,000 Haitians – president Fernández hailed the reforms a 'democratic revolution'.[33] The constitution enshrined changes from the 2004 Migration Law, introducing a new definition of the Dominican nationality. From this date, Dominicans were now regarded:

> ...persons born on national territory with the exception of the sons and daughters of members of diplomatic and consular legations, [and] foreigners who find themselves in transit or residing illegally on Dominican territory[34]

---

32. OBMICA, *Facilitando el acceso al registro civil dominicano a descendientes de parejas mixtas: protocolo para su acompañamiento legal* (Santo Domingo: OBMICA, 2018).
33. US Government Cable, *Fernandez's Priority: A New Constitution* (Santo Domingo: US Government Cable, 2008a).
34. Asamblea Nacional, *Capítulo V, De La Población Sección I De La Nacionalidad Artículo 18. – Nacionalidad*, 2010: 'Son dominicanas y dominicanos: Las personas nacidas en territorio nacional, con excepción de los hijos e hijas de extranjeros miembros

Figure 4 Police officers and security line up outside the Constitutional Tribunal headquarters in Santo Domingo. Credits: Lorena Espinoza Peña.

Beyond question, these constitutional changes explicitly targeted the Haitian-descended and ultimately ended their claims to Dominican citizenship. Despite assurances from Fernández that the reforms would not affect populations retrospectively, accusations of improper and discriminatory practices by civil registry officials continued. One such denunciation was the case of Juliana Deguis Pierre, whose appeal was presented to tribunal judges by the Socio-Cultural Movement of Haitian Workers (MOSCTHA). MOSCTHA contested the government's use of Resolution 012-07 as a justification for confiscating Deguis Pierre's birth certificate and denounced this as an abuse of her fundamental rights.[35] All but two of the judges rejected these claims.[36] They instead argued that Article 11 of the

---

de legaciones diplomáticas y consulares, de extranjeros que se hallen en tránsito o residan ilegalmente en territorio dominicano. Se considera persona en tránsito a toda extranjera o extranjero definido como tal en las leyes dominicanas', Constitución de la República Dominicana de 2010.

35. *Sentencia* TC/0168/13, *Referencia*.
36. Isabel Bonilla Hernández and Katia Miguelina Jiménez Martínez gave the two dissenting votes.

Haitian Constitution already confirmed Deguis Pierre's status as Haitian national.[37] They ascertained that because both her parents were Haitians, the decision would render neither Deguis Pierre nor any other individual of Haitian ancestry stateless. Ignoring the strong linguistic, cultural and familial ties Deguis Pierre already held with the Dominican Republic, the decision instead hinged on a fundamental disagreement between the plaintiff over her perceived legal identity as a Dominican and the state's refusal to recognise her as anything other than Haitian. In response, Deguis Pierre stated:

> I am 28 years old and [...] not once have I been there [Haiti]. I don't know what it's like [...] because I've never been there because I was born here.[38]

Having determined Deguis Pierre a 'foreigner in transit', the judges then ratified terminology from the recently modified 2010 Constitution into law, confirming that anyone born between 16 June 1929 and 18 April 2007 to a parent deemed 'in transit' or 'residing illegally' had no claim to birthright citizenship. Underlining the need to normalise these 'irregularities', the judges instructed the Interior Ministry and the Police (MIP), the Dominican Congress and the civil registry to provide a full audit to detect others who, like Deguis Pierre, they claimed had mistakenly been issued Dominican paperwork. The judges then ordered the launch of the National Regularization Plan for Foreigners (PNRE), which had been initially contemplated within the 2004 Migration Law to target undocumented migrants. In a perverse twist, the court granted Deguis Pierre temporary permission to remain in the Dominican Republic, ordering her to instead register as a Haitian national through this new 'Regularisation' Plan.[39]

---

37. The Haitian Constitution permitted dual citizenship only in 2012 when it made amendments to its 1987 constitution. Before this date, citizens were eligible only to a Haitian nationality and therefore could not possess another nationality.
38. The Haiti Support Group, *Stateless in the Caribbean: The Haiti Briefing*, 2014, 1.
39. 'CUARTO: DISPONER, asimismo, que la Dirección General de Migración, dentro del indicado plazo de diez (10) días, otorgue un permiso especial de estadía temporal en el país a la señora Juliana Dequis (o Deguis) Pierre, hasta que el Plan nacional de regularización de los extranjeros ilegales radicados en el país previsto en el artículo 151 de la Ley de Migración núm. 285-04 determine las condiciones de regularización de este género de casos'. See *Sentencia* TC/0168/13, *Referencia*.

Figure 5 The protests continue: 'We are as Dominican as you are.' Credits: Lorena Espinoza Peña.

The PLD had hoped that the 2013 *Sentencia* would quietly and discretely put an end to birthright citizenship provisions within the Dominican Constitution to ensure that, once and for all, people born to Haitian parents would be permanently excluded from recognition as Dominicans. Unexpectedly, news of the ruling erupted into mass controversy (Figure 5). The Dominican government received near-universal condemnation from human rights campaigners, international and domestic NGOs and statelessness experts who all reacted angrily to the enforcement of citizenship-stripping practices that ultimately rendered Deguis Pierre, and hundreds of thousands like her, without a nationality. The Caribbean Community CARICOM was particularly critical and swiftly suspended the Dominican Republic's application for membership to the organisation. The Institute on Statelessness and Inclusion called it

> the most egregious new violation of international human rights norms relating to nationality and statelessness that the world has witnessed in the 21st Century.[40]

---

40. ISI, *The World's Stateless* (Tilburg: Institute on Statelessness and Inclusion, 2014), 8.

In response to this fierce international criticism,[41] President Medina (elected as leader of the ruling PLD in 2012) promised the country would find a 'humanitarian solution to the crisis'.[42] Following intense negotiation between the Executive, the Ministry of Internal Affairs, the Chancellery, the civil registry and the far-right nationalist group FNP, this solution included the implementation of a legislative 'fix' known as Naturalisation Law 169-14. Passed by Congress on 12 May 2014 and implemented in late July the same year, the law provided a pathway to 'naturalisation' for those affected by the ruling. Effectively, this new law forced persons born in the Dominican Republic to present their cases to the state as a means of (re)claiming their citizenship. Law 169-14 divided people into two separate categories:

- Group A – registered nationals born in the Dominican Republic to 'undocumented' non-Dominican parents between 16 June 1929 and 18 April 2007. Persons in this group had the opportunity to 'regularise' their citizenship status with the civil registry (JCE). This process openly named and shamed people affected and made their details public via the JCE website and in a local newspaper.[43]
- Group B – native-born, foreign-descended individuals with no state-issued documentation. Persons in this category had to register as foreigners with the MIP and not the civil registry as Dominicans. In theory, this group would be given the opportunity to apply for naturalisation after a period of two years.[44]

---

41. Criticism came from CARICOM, the UNHCR, UNICEF, the United States, the European Union and others. See L. Gamboa and J. Harrington Reddy, 'Judicial denationalisation of Dominicans of Haitian Descent', *Forced Migration Review* 46 (2014).
42. Presidencia de la República Dominicana, *República Dominicana explica ante OEA estrategia regularización de extranjeros*, 2013.
43. On 26 June 2014, the JCE published the names of people in Group A audited by the JCE in the national newspaper *Listin Diario*. The document publicly named approximately fifty-five thousand people registered under the Naturalisation Plan, 43,000 of whom were persons of Haitian ancestry. See Junta Central Electoral, *Invitamos a todas las personas contenidas en este listado a pasar por las Oficialías del Estado Civil que aparecen en esta relación a recoger su acta de registro de inscripción que le acredita como dominicanos en virtud de la Ley No. 169/14, Listin Diario* (Santo Domingo: JCE, 2014).
44. At the time of writing, the 'naturalisation' process had yet to take place, nor was it clear to any of the Group B candidates I interviewed in Chapter 5 if they could (re)apply for citizenship as Dominicans following a period of two years. Human Rights Watch has already reported difficulties with the registrations. See Human Rights Watch, *We Are Dominican. Arbitrary Deprivation of Nationality in the Dominican Republic: Summary* (New York: Human Rights Watch, 2015).

The fallout from the 2013 *Sentencia* and the introduction of Naturalisation Law 169-14 imposed further cumbersome bureaucratic demands on Dominican citizens, tens of thousands of whom were mired in poverty and unable to meet the 'regularisation' criteria required by the Dominican authorities. The government promised that if Dominican-born applicants followed the correct procedures and submitted the required documentation, the civil registry would ensure they were issued with the corresponding legal identity documentation. Most people in Group A and Group B were already recognised within the constitution as Dominicans at the time of their birth but now faced increased scrutiny from registry officials to evidence the validity of their Dominican legal identity.

Reactions to the *Sentencia*

All the NGO practitioners and fieldworkers I spoke with told me the *Sentencia* was a complete shock to them. While in the past many had already encountered individual cases of statelessness, they said they were simply not prepared for the magnitude of the ruling nor the impact it would have on their communities. Prior to the *Sentencia*, the practitioners had worked directly with Haitian immigrants to help them declare and acquire birth certificates for their children. Afterwards, the panorama shifted completely as they focused primarily on helping adults who found it impossible to get their paperwork. All unequivocally saw persons of Haitian descent as Dominican citizens with the right to a legal identity. As one anonymous human rights activist noted:

> They are Dominicans, not foreigners. They were born here and recorded as Dominicans. Law 169-14 said that persons in Group A declared before 2007 could get their documents as Dominicans. For Group B, the government allowed these people to be declared as foreigners. After 2 years, they could apply to naturalise as Dominicans.

The people I spoke with saw documentation as a necessary component of nationality recognition. They regularly referred to a person without a birth certificate or with invalid or out-of-date paperwork as having no nationality or being stateless. They knew that, without their documents, life was much more complicated. The practitioners were knowledgeable about the practicalities associated with registrations and their potentially negative impact. They were frustrated and angry that decisions made by civil registry officials had created these problems in their communities.

After the introduction of Law 169-14, affected populations were perplexed by the demands placed upon them. Many did not understand what paperwork they needed or what they had to do to (re)obtain their documents. When the

Haitian-descended arrived at the JCE (civil registry) to get their Dominican paperwork, many found they were either turned away or given conflicting information. Not unsimilar to the problems development practitioners also alluded to, government officials were finding it difficult to differentiate between undocumented Dominicans and Haitians. As the anonymous activist I spoke with stated:

> They [the authorities] confuse Group B with Haitian immigrants. If you go with the piece of paper to the JCE [civil registry] they send you to immigration in Santo Domingo. There was a lot of confusion.

The fallout from the *Sentencia* and Law 169-14 resulted in chaotic scenes at the civil registry as officials turned people away who were trying to register in large groups. NGOs and lawyers were no longer allowed to accompany individuals. People with limited access to resources were expected to navigate complex bureaucratic systems without any form of legal representation.

To learn more about the NGO battle to push for the legal recognition of the Haitian-descended, I spoke with Dr Bridget Wooding, director of the Caribbean Migrants Observatory (OBMICA) and an academic who has worked with Haitian migrants since the 1980s. Dr Wooding has written extensively about the problems facing migrant-descended populations and is a prominent campaigner on statelessness. She referred to the state's reluctance to address the problem of under-registration as the *avestruz* ('ostrich') policy as for decades the authorities had been leaving their head in the sand and did not want to directly tackle the problem.

Dr Wooding noted how, by the mid-2000s, NGOs had won a space with the Inter-American system. At this time, many thought they were making progress and improving dialogue with the state. She told me about the dehumanising impact of government policy on populations struggling to obtain their paperwork and how NGOs began using strategic litigation and jurisprudence through the Inter-American system and domestic courts as an advocacy tool to campaign against the human rights violations facing children born to Haitian migrants.

Dominican NGOs had been increasingly vocal about problems in accessing documentation yet had chosen to prioritise their engagement with international actors rather than strategise directly with the state.[45]

---

45. These actors included the UNHCR, the Center for Justice and International Law (CEJIL), Open Society and the Robert F. Kennedy Center for Justice and Human Rights, among others.

OBMICA's focus remained firmly fixed on stateless populations: Haitian migrants together with their Dominican-born children living in precarity along the border and in *bateyes*. Dr Wooding saw the post-2013 'regularisation' drives as a space for constructive engagement and a shift towards greater formality. She said that while angry about the wide-reaching impact of the *Sentencia*, many in civil society accepted Law 169-14 as a means of partially remediating the initial fallout from the ruling. They knew they would need to cooperate with the state.

Nevertheless, others were wholly dissatisfied with the situation and angry about the implementation of this new law. I met with Ana María Belique Delba, a human rights activist, child of Haitian parents and employee of Centro Bonó, a religious NGO that has campaigned for years for the rights of Haitian-descended populations to a Dominican nationality. Belique Delba considered the registration drives introduced as part of Law 169-14 an additional, unnecessary and discriminatory layer of bureaucracy. She said:

As citizens, we are being made to jump through hoops

Belique Delba is founder of Reconoci.do, a campaign group formed to highlight the bureaucratic difficulties facing documented persons of Haitian descent. Initially, Reconoci.do worked exclusively with people already registered with the authorities (Group A). She told me they were reluctant to associate with persons with no form of documentation (Group B) because she saw the two groups as very different from one another. Belique Delba said she was deeply unhappy about what she viewed as a truncation of citizenship rights for people, like her, who had already complied with the law, had their paperwork and had grown up as 'good' citizens. She stated:

They [the state] say that since we were born until the new constitution was modified, we are not Dominicans. They changed the rules of the game.

When I met with Belique Delba, she had a *caso de amparo* – a case on the grounds of unconstitutionality – pending against the Dominican state.[46] The civil registry had already confiscated her Dominican ID card, which had left her in a precarious position and unable to access basic services. Belique Delba was adamant that she had always done things the 'right' way, arguing that documented (Group A) and undocumented (Group B) were two entirely

---

46. Suprema Corte de Justicia, *Junta Central Electoral v. Ana María Belique Delba. Resolución 1342-2014*, Santo Domingo, 2014.

different sets of people. She saw the additional bureaucratic demands placed upon citizens to prove their state membership unfair and discriminatory, reasoning that if she had always had her documents then she should not be treated in the same way as people without their documents. She belonged to the system, she said, and always played by the rules yet saw herself overwhelmingly treated like a foreigner. This had a significant impact on how she felt about her own identity and sense of belonging. She told me:

> I am still a Dominican because I was Dominican the day I came into this world. But what makes you Dominican? A person is where they are born. It is not just what the law says. I can't identify with Haiti. I don't have the Haitian culture in me. I have been there now through a process of exploration. But they see me as a foreigner even though here they want to say I am Haitian. I learnt some *kreyòl* but a Haitian hears me speaking and they know it's a foreigner speaking their language. Everything I am I have learnt here. The way I am, the way I think. There are attitudes and ways of being. I am an expression of what I see: history, language, traditions, food, dance, music, religion. Practically everything. I can't give you one specific example. It's a combination of things.

Belique Delba noted how difficulties in obtaining citizenship documents made social ascent much more difficult. She said that this is why legal identity was so valuable to children born to Haitians. It was their way out of the plantation and the door to a better life. Dominicans of Haitian ancestry had aspirations and wanted to branch out into other areas, which is why they needed their documentation, she argued:

> While NGOs and the media focus on the deportations of Haitian migrants, in reality practices that block access to documentation are intended as a means to keep populations like ours in our place. It's not about sending us 'back' to a place we supposedly came from, it's to make sure we never move up the social scale or leave the *batey*.

In the next chapter, we will hear from migrant-descended Dominicans of different socioeconomic backgrounds and of various national and ethnic origins about their experiences of the nationwide registrations introduced after the *Sentencia* as part of Law 169-14. We will learn about their interactions with civil registry officials, the steps they had to take and if they were successful in acquiring their new Dominican biometric ID card. Analysis of these experiences is important because, following the fallout from the *Sentencia*, and facing increased international scrutiny, the Dominican civil registry (JCE) took the decision to quietly drop the racial categorisations of *negro, mulato, blanco, indio* (among others) which, since the 1930s, had been a major feature of the Dominican national ID card. The chapter will therefore expose some of the more insidious and hidden methods the authorities were able to incorporate to racially discriminate against Black Dominicans, the Haitian-descended and others. We will explore the myriad of ways, some positive, some negative and some surprisingly inconsequential, that Dominicans have experienced contemporary legal identity practices as well as their impact on their perceptions of their own identity, belonging and national status. This includes transnational populations who found themselves in an incredibly difficult predicament while living overseas and unable to renew their Dominican passport.

Chapter 5

DOMINICAN OR NOT DOMINICAN? CITIZENS AND THEIR EXPERIENCES OF LEGAL IDENTITY MEASURES

> When there is such a negation of Blackness [...] when someone has Black features [...] they are seen as Haitian [...] even when the person has no connection whatsoever with Haiti.[1]

Until this book, studies that examined the impact of the *Sentencia* focused primarily on the experiences of persons already living at the *fringes* of citizenship.[2] Namely, undocumented stateless populations – often children – born in the Dominican Republic to Haitian migrants who, because they had no birth certificate, could not access their Dominican nationality.[3] In this chapter, we will expand this approach further to consider the experiences of people the anthropologist Samuel Martínez refers to as the 'un-Dominicans'.[4] These are individuals who exist in law as *citizens* yet have faced overwhelmingly convoluted bureaucratic and administrative obstacles when attempting to acquire state-issued paperwork.

To provoke debate and encourage new modes of thinking about the Dominican case, I argued in Chapter 2 for the need to *dehaitianise* our approaches to the *Sentencia*. This, I maintain, is to help us understand how citizenship-stripping practices, while motivated by anti-Haitianism, form part of a broader *destabilising* process (Aber and Small, 2013) which is experienced across the body politic in different and sometimes contradictory ways. While the actions of the Dominican state have been indisputably and unforgivably discriminatory towards persons of Haitian ancestry, in this chapter we will also consider the ways in which efforts to provide all Dominicans with their

---

1. A man born to Haitian parents recorded in Group A as part of Law 169-14.
2. B. N. Lawrance and J. Stevens, *Citizenship in Question: Evidentiary Birthright and Statelessness*, ed. J. S. Benjamin and N. Lawrance (Durham: Duke University Press, 2017).
3. These are individuals classified in Law 169-14 as Group B individuals.
4. S. Martínez, 'Anti-Haitian Exclusionism in the Dominican Republic', YouTube video, Center for Religion, Ethics and Culture, 2015.

legal identity through the issuance of the new biometric ID card have affected Black Dominicans of no immediate foreign ancestry, Black Dominicans of Anglo-Caribbean descent (*cocolos*), and other Dominicans of non-Haitian ancestry,[5] including two women I interviewed for this chapter who were born to Japanese and Argentinean parents.

This approach moves in line with the sociologist Tonkiss and the political theorist Bloom who support the need to interpret noncitizenship beyond a legalistic and rights-based lens to instead see it as a 'heterogeneous and complex' construct experienced empirically in a variety of ways (2015, p. 844). For the purposes of this book, I interpret these as an 'assemblage' of measures (Goldring and Landolt, 2013) that can cast doubt and uncertainty over how citizens access their legal identity and the demands placed upon them to evidence their right to belong. By amplifying the voices of the un-Dominican, I will highlight the tensions with contemporary understandings of the assumed inclusionary impact of legal identity practices for all citizens and how these are experienced empirically (Bhabha and Robinson, 2011).

As we have seen, policymakers, NGOs and academics frame the 2013 *Sentencia* within the context of Haitian migration into the Dominican Republic and cross-border bi-national Haitian-Dominican relations, looking mainly to the *batey* (sugar plantation) and the border to carry out ethnographic research. In an effort to broaden our understandings of the scope and scale of the *Sentencia*, and the impact of subsequent registrations to provide all Dominicans with a biometric ID card, I travelled the length and breadth of the island. I met with informants from a range of socioeconomic, national and ethnic backgrounds who have had to (re)negotiate and navigate complex state architectures and bureaucracies to prove their right to belong. I purposely spoke with documented citizens who already held some form of legal identity paperwork, including informants living overseas. We will see how many of these experiences directly conflict with the current assumptions of policymakers and international development organisations regarding the

---

5. In total, I spoke with fifteen informants of immediate foreign descent whose parents were born in another country and had migrated to the Dominican Republic. I easily identified nine persons in Group A via a list the JCE had published in a local newspaper. They included six persons of Haitian descent, two of Argentinean descent and one of Japanese descent. Each Group A informant already held a state-issued identity card but had faced obstacles in renewing this document before the introduction of the new law. All of the informants of Haitian descent had been registered with a *ficha*, a work permit given to Haitians on sugar cane plantations. Constitutional Tribunal judges challenged the validity of this document as part of the *Sentencia*. None were recorded using a Dominican ID number hence (I concluded) why their files had been flagged up on the government database.

inclusionary nature of legal identity practices. This includes persons who, before the introduction of recent legal identity practices, would never have imagined that the state could challenge the validity or authenticity of their right to a Dominican legal identity.

Persons of No Immediate Foreign Ancestry

I travelled to San José de las Matas (Figure 6), a rural town in the north-west of the country, to meet with a 42-year-old mother of three. The informant, a *Solidaridad* (state welfare) beneficiary, worked in agriculture selling avocados. She spoke positively about the benefits of recent registration drives. She told me how representatives began arriving in her community, visiting one house-hold to the next. She recalled that on at least five separate occasions, people had arrived at her house to record details about her home and her family. They also spoke to her friends and neighbours in the village asking similar questions. She said she did not know why they were doing this and assumed the information was for the national census.

Figure 6 San José de las Matas, Santiago Province. Credits: author.

The informant had held two ID cards in her lifetime: the old paper ID, which she recently updated for the new biometric version as part of the registrations. She did not see her identity card as particularly important but was told that she needed one to ensure that she would be included into the *Solidaridad* programme. When I asked her about the advantages of this new ID document, she stated:

> Well, I need the new ID to use my *Solidaridad* card. And to go to the hospital. You always use your ID there. I use the card about once a month. You go and give it to the *colmado* [local convenience store] and they give you food. […] You need your ID to get the [welfare] card. […] They use a machine in the *colmado* when you buy things. A lot of *colmados* have the machine now.

The machine she referred to was a *Solidaridad* card machine endorsed by Visa. The only way to access benefits was by obtaining a *cédula* then using this to acquire the new electronic welfare card. The informant could no longer use cash. She saw this as an exciting and modern change. Having the card made her feel like a member of the community, she told me. She also recalled the efforts of civil society, local NGOs, the Catholic Church and the state to encourage everyone in her village to register. She had heard announcements on the radio. A priest had told his congregation about the new registration drives during mass. People in the community had said how important it would be for her to update her ID to receive welfare. As part of the new registration drives, she was sent to see a civil registry official who verified her details on a computer. After two weeks, she received a phone call to confirm that she could go and collect her new ID. The informant said she was happy and found the process straightforward enough. She reported no major issues in obtaining her Dominican ID or *Solidaridad* welfare card.

I then travelled to Tamayo, Bahoruco, in the south-west of the country to meet with a domestic worker whose background was similar to that of the woman in San José de las Matas. Her experience of registrations was very different and she was facing seemingly insurmountable hurdles in her attempts to obtain a birth certificate for her young son. Her parents and grandparents were both documented Dominican citizens.[6] When she went to renew her papers, a civil registry official told her that her file was flagging up an error on the computer system. To resolve this, she had to travel to the capital Santo

---

6. I was shown the Dominican national identity cards of the informant, her father and grandfather that corroborated this statement.

Domingo. The journey took her several hours and was costly. She said she did not know what to do about the situation and was worried about the impact it was having on her family. The woman said it was very stressful and led her to argue with her father and her family.

There was an evident racial dimension to this woman's story. She had no recorded Haitian ancestry but said that sometimes she was treated as a Haitian because, she reasoned, of her dark skin colour. She told me how she had started to encounter difficulties when trying to renew her documentation in the town. A civil registry official kept sending her back and forth to the capital and she was finding it impossible to resolve the issue. The woman showed me a letter from one civil registry official who stated that he had ordered an investigation to determine her 'true' nationality (Figure 7). The letter said:

> Honourable Magistrate,
>
> I, the undersigned, Civil Registry Official from the Municipality of Tamayo, wish to draw your attention to the following matter, with the aim of determining the true nationality of the lady […], bearer of the Identity Card and Electoral Number […], who is attempting to declare her son, yet appears to be of foreign nationality, for which we are carrying out this request for the corresponding purposes.

The informant was underage when she had her first child and was able to register the birth at the hospital using a *cédula de menor*.[7] By the time her third child was born in 2015, she was given a pink form from the hospital (*Constancia de Nacido Vivo*).[8] She was instructed to take this to the civil registry. She took this piece of paper and her ID to collect the birth certificate. A registry official in her town subsequently told her that he could not register her child due to a problem with her 'foreign-sounding' last name. Her case, she was informed, was being reviewed and would take a number of days to resolve. Three months later, the informant was still trying to get an update and could not understand why it was so difficult to register her son. She told me she was confused about why she was experiencing these problems now when her two other children already had their Dominican birth certificate. Her father had never encountered any problems, nor had any of her siblings. She wanted an explanation for what was happening.

The informant did not understand why her Dominican nationality was being challenged or how an anomaly like this might have appeared on her file.

---

7. This is an identity card issued to young mothers who are under the age of 16 so they can register their child.
8. This is the document given to the mother of a newborn child to confirm their personal details, including the date of birth. Pink for foreign child, white for Dominican.

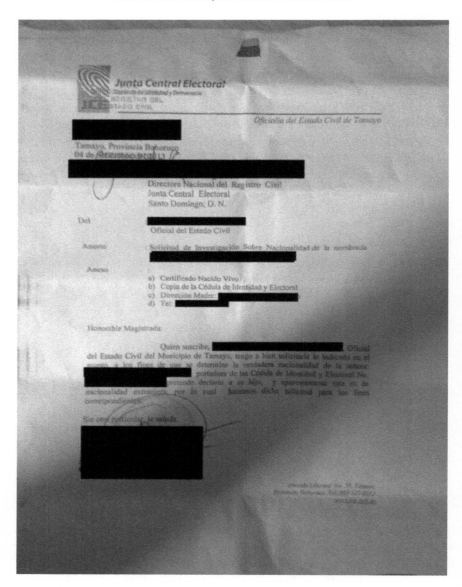

Figure 7 Letter from the civil registry querying the validity of the Dominican nationality of a documented woman of non-Haitian ancestry. Credits: author.

She reasoned it must have been the fault of the civil registry official who wrote the letter. She did not see this as a systemic problem, but a personal one. She said the official in her town recognises and knows her. She saw it as a form of abuse and a personal attack. He was in a position of power and had chosen to create problems for her, she said.

As we concluded the interview, the woman was unclear about her next steps. She said she had never really thought much about what being Dominican meant to her. Now, she feels differently as she is not the person she thought she once was. Her entire family is Dominican, but the civil registry is telling her that she is foreign. She wanted to get a birth certificate for her son and find a practical solution to the problem as quickly as possible. She was worried for her future and that of the child she was struggling to register.

Documented Persons of Haitian Descent (Group 'A')

I remained in the south of the country and travelled to a *batey* near Bahoruco to meet with the owner of a local grocery store (*colmado*). This first informant I spoke with had Haitian grandparents and had grown up in the *batey* with his siblings and Dominican-born parents. We talked at length about the practical difficulties of living in the *batey* and finding work. The *colmado* owner lamented the lack of educational opportunities for children in the *batey*. Although they had access to a primary education, the secondary school was much further away, and most families from the *batey* could not afford to send their children there. Families, he told me, needed a lot of dynamism and strength to move forward in life.

As the owner of a *colmado*, the man occupied an important social position within his community. His experience differed greatly from that of the majority of persons of Haitian descent interviewed in this section. He had experienced no difficulties accessing his legal identity, showing me a valid identity card, driving licence and passport. He stated, nevertheless, that he was acutely aware of the problems many of his friends, neighbours and customers were facing, specifically people like him who were of Haitian descent.

The man interacted daily with his customers, including *Solidaridad* welfare beneficiaries. He told me how they would go to his store and use the card to electronically buy the basic goods they needed for their families. Cash was becoming a thing of the past, he said.

For those who had managed to acquire their ID, life was much easier. The situation had become impossible for others. Every day he encountered customers who complained they could not renew their ID to claim welfare or get healthcare assistance as they had done in the past. He made a very clear connection between an increased emphasis on the need for documentation and the ability of Haitian-descended populations to rise up the social scale, noting:

> The Vicini family [an influential and affluent sugar-producing Dominican family of Italian heritage] [...] they think they know what being Dominican means but I think they are mistaken. They talk about sovereignty. But if I can't be in the country because I am a Dominican of Haitian descent then neither can they. They are as much foreigners as I am. This applies to others too [...] Consuelo Despradel [a right-wing TV and radio personality] and the Cardinal [known for his vehemently pro-Hispanic, anti-Haitian stance]. People who support their cause. *Dominicanidad* is not just about pride. It is about seeing others who are losing their nationality.

The man was acutely aware of the value of paperwork for people in his community. He knew that he was the exception to the rule. Those without ID could not access healthcare or welfare and were effectively stuck. He linked these to socioeconomic problems and issues with race. It was clear for him that there was one rule for the rich, particularly when of European descent. He added:

> We are pushing them [people of Haitian descent] into a social limbo. There are children who can't study. Because of this attack, they can't move upwards. For people who don't have their documents, they are not insured. They can't even go to a clinic to be treated. They can't get hold of a *Solidaridad* card and they don't have an insurance card. They [the Vicinis] don't experience any of this because they have the money, influence and social status.

These comments echoed the views of Ana Belique from the activist group Re.conocido who I interviewed in the previous chapter. They both saw papers as a means to leave the *batey* and climb up the social ladder. Without them, the *colmado* owner was concerned that Haitian-descended populations would remain trapped within the plantation in precarious jobs. He said that his neighbours and friends were being treated as second-class citizens and the situation clearly upset him. Crucially, they both said the *Sentencia* was not about expulsing the Haitian-descended or deporting migrants across the border; it was a strategy to keep populations in their place as a form of exploitable, and undetectable, labour.

From Bahoruco I travelled to a *batey* in nearby Cristóbal, where I began to learn about some of the absurdities Haitian-descended populations were encountering in their interactions with the civil registry. This second informant I spoke with told me that his grandparents had migrated to the Dominican Republic from Haiti. He had started school aged 9 but did not finish his primary education. At 17, he began working at a free trade zone (FTZ) in the tourist town of La Romana, which opened up a lot of new opportunities to him, allowing him to travel abroad, including a contract in South Korea with a textiles company. The man noted how easy it used to be to get this identity card and passport. He underlined the opportunities his ID card had opened up for him, telling me:

> That document – my old card – it meant that I could travel. It meant that I could work.

From 2010, the informant in Cristóbal began to encounter major problems with the registrations process. He noted, for example, that lawyers were no longer allowed to accompany their clients to the civil registry to help them with their documents. Although his Dominican-born parents had recorded his birth using the father's ID card, local officials told him they could not locate the number of this document within the registry. As a result, they requested he provide a copy of his mother's Dominican birth certificate. When he could not produce this document, he was sent to the JCE in Santo Domingo. He said he was made to travel over five times to the capital at considerable expense to his person. Although a nuisance, he was eventually able to prove that his mother was indeed a Dominican.

In 2014, the informant went to renew his *cédula* as part of the new registrations. Once again, a registry official told him his file presented *inconvenientes* (problems). The reasons, however, were different this time. Firstly, the system had flagged up an error with a misspelling in his first name. Secondly, it found that his *cédula* mistakenly stated that he was a woman. He laughed about this situation saying he did not understand why it was such an issue now. In the past, state officials had overlooked the error, and he even managed to get a passport that correctly stated he was a man.[9] He was concerned that, because of these issues, he would not meet the deadline for his ID renewal, and this would affect his ability to vote in the 2016 presidential elections. He was extremely happy when officials corrected his details and gave him a new card with the correct name and gender. He was also grateful that he could

---

9. The impact of the *Sentencia* and registrations on non-binary and transgender people as well other groups who do not fit comfortably within this neoliberal, heteronormative framework would make a rich and fascinating case study, particularly if it focused on the intersections between race, class and gender.

get this card for free. He nevertheless criticised the additional costs involved with resolving these issues. The return journey to the capital cost 600 pesos each time he travelled. He also had to wake up very early to ensure that he could arrive at the JCE on time. It cost over 200 pesos each time he needed to legalise his documents or renew his birth certificate. He stated:

> You need a *cédula* to get around. If someone wants to make life difficult they can if you don't have one. In some places, they were no longer accepting the old ID card and that began to create some difficulties for me.

His comment showed how the centralisation of services through the national identity card rendered the card essential for both social and financial inclusion. This, he feared, meant that it could be misused to create problems for some people. He told me how each time he went to the bank, he found it harder to withdraw money. Sometimes he used his driving licence as identification even though he knew he really should have shown his ID card. When asked how he negotiated the situation, he said he had a personal contact there who helped him. For over a year, he had trouble accessing remittances sent from abroad via Western Union. The staff would not accept his old ID. He told me he was much happier after the recent registrations as he was able to get his new card. Life, he assured me, was going to get much more manageable from hereon in.

To reach the third informant, a 52-year-old woman, I travelled to Guaymate, which is located in the Yuma region to the north of the tourist town of La Romana. My interview in Guaymate highlighted the problem of Haitian-descended populations who had received ID cards during election periods. As we have seen, politicians would travel to the *bateyes* to hand out ID cards as a way to win votes for their parties. Many of the people who were given papers were never formally registered and therefore had no official birth certificate. While those in this group assumed that this ID served as confirmation of their Dominican citizenship, the civil registry began annulling their papers on the grounds that there was no formal record of their legal existence. The problem was compounded further because they were told they needed to produce evidence of a Dominican birth certificate from their mother or father, and either many could not find this document or it did not exist because their parents were Haitian.

This woman's great-grandparents were from Haiti, and her parents and grandparents were born in the Dominican Republic in a nearby *batey*. She recounted how, in the 1970s, representatives from the authoritarian leader Balaguer's Social Christian Reformist Party (PRSC) would visit the area. In those days, it was very easy for both Haitian migrants and Dominicans to obtain state-issued Dominican paperwork from vote-hungry politicians:

> All people had to do was look at you, and they would give you an ID card. It was not that difficult for Haitians or Dominicans to get hold of.

That situation had now radically changed. The woman told me that before 2011 she did not worry too much about her papers. She only recently ran into serious difficulties when trying to graduate from a nearby secondary school. The woman subsequently sought the help of a local judge and an NGO platform. They asked for a copy of her mother's birth and death certificate and ID card as well as a record of her baptism. The NGOs also helped her travel a very long distance to her birth town of Baní in the southwest of the country to request the originals of her documents. Although she had initially encountered problems, with their support she was able to deposit her papers and ensure that her details were recorded within the system.

The fourth informant I spoke with was a 25-year-old man from a nearby *batey*, Los Tocones, who now lived in the centre of La Romana with his Haitian 'wife'[10] and her 10-year-old child. In direct contradiction with the claims of policymakers that documentation can be transformative and life altering, the man said that he had no strong feelings about this. He saw the process as a big inconvenience and a means to an end. The man also told me that he did not mind how he was registered, as either a Dominican or a Haitian. Instead, he said that identity disputes had gotten in the way of him being able to live his life the way he wanted. Overall, he was apathetic about the entire process and was tired with the inefficiency of the system.

The man was known to a lot of people in the town because he worked at a local discotheque. He worked in the informal economy and was always paid in cash so, he reasoned, was not overly motivated to get his new ID. Instead he told me he needed the card because he had already had numerous negative encounters with the authorities, which included systematic racial abuse. The man complained that the police regularly stopped him to ask for

---

10. When a person talks about 'marriage' in this context, oftentimes they mean that they are co-habiting (*amancebado*) with their partner, not that they have formally participated in a wedding ceremony which would imply they received documentation to evidence their married status. This observation matters because even if a woman has lived for a very long time with the father to her children, this lack of formal marital status would affect how the couple register their offspring.

his papers. When they saw him in the street, they would tease him about his Afro hair, which he referred to as his 'flow'.[11] 'Sometimes they pulled it', he told me.

The informant was put in jail on at least five separate occasions because he could not provide documents for the police. He said he resented being locked up for several hours with criminals when he was a law-abiding citizen. He even sold his motorbike and had to borrow money to travel to the capital so that he could get his papers. When he arrived at the civil registry, an official refused to take his picture for his ID. He was told to cut off his Afro hair, which, he said, was a big part of his identity and very important to him. The informant also complained that the process was tiring. He first had to get a copy of his father's birth certificate. He said he was not happy about this at all. He was irritated about the problems he was facing because he could not produce an ID card upon demand and was angry that he was forced to change his appearance to conform to the system.

The man saw this situation as deeply unfair. Despite being from the same family, born to the same parents and having lived at the same address, the man and his two brothers had wildly different experiences of registrations, a situation he saw as utterly absurd. As he told me, he had a Dominican birth certificate but no identity card and was publicly named in Group A as part of Law 169-14 following the *Sentencia*. This meant that he had to make a number of trips back and forth to the capital to have his file reviewed and his Dominican identity interrogated and 'verified' by a registry official. This had led to negative encounters with the authorities who would treat him badly because of his appearance. Contradictorily, the second brother had obtained his ID with complete ease. He was approached by a baseball representative from the United States who had intervened and paid for him to get a passport so that he could travel abroad on a sports scholarship. The third brother was in the most precarious position as he had no form of documentation whatsoever. As he had never formally been declared, the town's mayor told him he would have to register as a Haitian national if he wanted some form of paperwork. Each of the three brothers therefore had had radically different interactions with the authorities. The first brother – the informant – encountered numerous difficulties including racial harassment from the police – but eventually managed to retain his Dominican status. The intervention of a baseball scout from the United States meant that the second brother never had his Dominican citizenship challenged or questioned. The third brother faced so many problems that he was told to register as a Haitian and eventually gave up even trying to get his Dominican ID.

---

11. His fashion sense and style.

When I asked the informant how he felt about this situation, he told me he found it completely ridiculous. He said it did not matter to him what his papers said. He might have a Dominican ID, but he was also proud of his Haitian roots. Now that he had his documents, he noted, it would be easier to study, but apart from that, he saw little use for the card. He was clearly very irritated by the problems he and his family had faced.

The fifth informant of Haitian descent I spoke with was born to Haitian parents in a *batey* near the sugar-producing town of San Pedro de Macorís. A lack of access to paperwork had caused the man great turmoil in his job as a lawyer particularly because he was living overseas when the state began to introduce new legal identity measures.[12] A state official at the Dominican embassy refused to renew his passport, resulting in considerable distress. He had a valid visa from the country he was living in but struggled to get a new Dominican passport. Without this document, he was left stateless and unable to travel.

The man told me that for years he had chosen to hide his Haitian origins from his friends and colleagues. He worked in the public sector and had regularly represented his country at events abroad. He heard his colleagues make derogatory comments about Haitians and had tried to protect himself, keeping his own roots a secret from others. It was only when his name was published in Group A in the national newspaper that his colleagues and friends found out that his parents were Haitian, and this began to create difficulties for him. The informant articulated with great clarity the ambiguity of race in the Dominican imagination and how he could hide his origins from others. He told me:

> When there is such a negation of Blackness [...] when someone has Black features [...] they are seen as Haitian [...] even when the person has no connection whatsoever with Haiti. [...] When people see that you have no accent and you speak Spanish exactly the same way as them, when they see you are educated and you behave in a certain way [...] people don't associate you with Haiti. They completely remove the notion that you could be Haitian or of Haitian origin from their head. For them, this comes as a surprise. The automatic response is always: 'How is that possible? You don't act like you're Haitian.'

The man recounted how, when he was a child, there was not a strong culture of registering children, especially in rural areas. He had seen how the need for documentation had increased since his childhood when, at the age

---

12. I have chosen not to divulge more details about where he is living to protect his identity.

of 11, nuns visited his *batey* to help the children register. His town was popular with the opposition party, the PRD. He reasoned that to the ruling PLD an ID card was seen as the loss of a vote. That was the real reason why children born to Haitians found it so hard to get their documents, he said.

From the age of 18 onwards, the man began to encounter serious problems that, he stated, had a detrimental and overwhelming impact on his person and his career. He insisted that, without the help of his friends, personal contacts and political connections, he would never have been able to sort out his predicament. Whereas the previous informant who worked in the informal economy, was paid in cash and largely saw the ID card as a massive inconvenience, this man needed his documents to continue practicing law. He said that he understood how the law worked and had even gotten into an argument with registry officials who told him that, as the son of Haitians, he was not eligible for an ID card. He told me that many of the people who participated in the registrations process were lawyers; some were his colleagues and friends. They knew that what the state was doing was an infraction of people's rights, yet at the same time they had benefitted financially from helping to implement the registrations.

In the mid-2000s, the informant secured a state-sponsored scholarship to study for a master's degree in Europe. He returned to his village to request a certified copy of his birth certificate for acceptance onto this scheme. A civil registry official told him she had received an order not to give paperwork to people 'like him'. He said he was then sent to the capital to try and resolve the matter. He told me he felt frustrated, powerless and vulnerable. When he arrived in the capital, he demanded to speak to a senior civil registry official. This led to a heated, near-violent confrontation during which they argued about the constitution.[13] He told them they were violating his rights and needed to do their job correctly. The official told the informant he was not Dominican because his parents were Haitian. At this point, he became really upset and angry. The dispute ended with the official calling a lieutenant to take him away. Following this experience, the man said he used his political contacts to secure two copies of his birth certificate. A friend with political connections accompanied him to the passport office to get his travel document. Without these contacts, he told me, he never would have been able to secure his legal identity or travel abroad.

Frustratingly, the introduction of the new registration drives once again saw him battling with the authorities. Only this time he was already living abroad.

---

13. This was prior to changes introduced to the 2010 Constitution. The informant and the civil registry official disputed the constitutional definition of nationality and who were defined as Dominicans, specifically who should be defined as 'in transit'.

Immigration officials confronted him when he arrived at the airport in Santo Domingo. An official stopped him and said he suspected he was travelling on a false Dominican passport. When the man tried to renew his papers at the embassy, an official said he was awaiting authorisation from the civil registry and the passport office to sign and stamp his document, and until then, he could not give him his travel documents. He said he felt powerless, trapped and abused. The situation left him in a complete limbo as he could not go anywhere or travel back to the island until he could determine a solution to the problem.

The man said that his consistent ill-treatment made much more sense to him once he saw his name on the Group A list published in 2014 and realised that the system had flagged up his case. He spoke positively about the process, saying it was fairly straightforward. He was able to get a new ID card which now worked and allowed him to vote. He was nevertheless concerned that the authorities had publicly named and shamed him and about the impact this could have on his social standing. He reasoned that his parents were Haitian, but he had learnt Dominican values. His family had integrated into society. They grew up in a *batey*, but his father was a tailor, not a cane cutter. He always ensured his children had access to an education. The man also thought that because he had a good job and was educated, people did not associate him with Haiti:

I had a Dominican girlfriend once at university who asked me what my surname was. When I told her I had a Haitian last name, she didn't believe me. I had to sit down with her and talk about who I was and where my parents came from. Even when I see myself as Black and am proud of my Haitian origins, they see me as *indio*. As something other than Haitian.

The informant said that it was only through the new drives that his Haitian past had been brought to the fore. Whereas in the past his friends and colleagues had seen him as a Dominican, now they were starting to see him as a Haitian. He recognised that his identity was being manipulated and utilised for political gain. He said there were groups in power who wanted to maintain an anti-Haitian conversation to control and defend certain interests. He noted how ambiguous and conflictive this was, saying that the former dictator Trujillo had killed Dominicans for their physical appearance and the authoritarian leader Balaguer had deported people with no link to Haiti. He said that rich Dominicans all thought they were Europeans but that he strongly identified with his Dominican identity. He was born in the country and speaks Spanish. He had represented the government as a Dominican at international events.

How could it be that, when abroad, the state was happy to parade him around to other diplomats and foreign officials as a (Black) Dominican, but when back on the island, they treated him so poorly? He said he knew that his identity was being used for political advantage, as a way of challenging accusations of state racism. He lamented this situation, saying that *dominicanidad* was, in many ways, a denial of people's own Blackness and their African roots.

The final man I spoke with was born in La Romana but grew up in Marigot, in the south-east of Haiti. We conducted the interview in Haitian *kreyòl*. He showed me a copy of his Dominican birth certificate. As he had not lived in the country long enough, he never obtained a Dominican ID. A family member contacted him when he was in Haiti to tell him about the registrations taking place as part of Law 169-14. His mother, who was still living in the Dominican Republic, went to the civil registry to speak with officials and to try and get a copy of his birth certificate. He knew that the registrations were important and had heard about them on the radio. The man had neither a Haitian nor a Dominican passport, hiding in the back of a vehicle and crossing the border into the Dominican Republic in the middle of the night to avoid detection. He had already visited the civil registry four times only to be told that his information was not yet available on the system. He said he was motivated to get his Dominican identity card as it would facilitate access to better work and educational opportunities. He was still waiting to hear from the civil registry regarding his official status when we spoke.

Undocumented Persons of Haitian Descent (Group 'B')

Through the *Sentencia* ruling 168-13 and subsequent Law 169-14, the Dominican state administratively (re)categorised unregistered persons born in the Dominican Republic to two Haitian parents as foreign migrants. All the informants I spoke with in this section were living in rural areas in extreme poverty. No official record of them existed, and the civil registry had no evidence of their legal existence. There was no way I could corroborate whether everyone I spoke with had been born in the Dominican Republic or in Haiti. Instead, I was interested in learning about their experiences of the registrations particularly because the state had retroactively (re)labelled them as domestic-born Haitians. Persons in this group were forced to register through the Regularisation Plan for Foreigners in an Irregular Migratory Situation in the Dominican Republic (PNRE), which was introduced in 2014 after the *Sentencia*.

This first interview highlights the level of confusion experienced by many vulnerable populations about the registration drives. The woman was born in Sabana Grande de Boyá, an important site as it was the focus of the

Inter-American ruling we examined in Chapter 4. The informant told me that her Haitian parents had lost all their paperwork during Hurricane Georges.[14] She first heard about the registrations from the television in her local grocery store and went to the maternity ward to try, unsuccessfully, to collect her hospital birth records. The woman said she knew that because she held no form of paperwork, and to comply with the new rules, she would have to ask seven witnesses to confirm that she was born in the country in accordance with the PNRE. She travelled back and forth and was given a slip of paper with a registration number to call for an update. She said the process was very long, her papers were not yet ready and it cost her money each time she called for information. She told me, 'I still don't have my paperwork. They didn't give me anything.'

The woman said that she could not go to the hospital and had to pay to be seen by a doctor. While the documented man born to Haitian parents in the previous section said he identified as a Dominican, this woman saw herself as a Haitian. She needed a Dominican document because it would help her continue her studies, look after her children and give them a better life, she said. She was still unable to register her children and was still awaiting confirmation of her application status.

The second woman I spoke with did have a Dominican birth certificate and so in theory should have registered as a Dominican citizen. Nevertheless, she presented herself at the MIP and mistakenly registered as a Haitian. Her case highlights the confusion around registrations especially for income-poor populations. The woman, who lived in a *batey* in the east of the country, told me that she had found the whole process utterly confusing but wanted to do the 'right' thing. She had heard rumours from her neighbours that any person without the correct paperwork would be sent to Haiti. This scared her a lot. She told me she had gone to school but did not get very far. At the age of 15, she got 'married' to her Haitian 'husband'. The couple had two girls, a 6- and a 2-year-old. The man worked in construction in the tourist town of Bávaro on the east of the island, but he also cut cane so that they could continue to live in the *batey*.

The woman's parents were both Haitian, and she was born in the *batey*. She told me that her parents registered her when she was born. She had a Dominican birth certificate but said that getting an ID *estaba dando brega* ('it was hard work'). She took her Dominican birth certificate to the civil registry in Guaymate with the help of a neighbour. The woman was told that she

---

14. Hurricane Georges had a devastating on the Dominican Republic when it hit in 1998. It killed close to four hundred people and had a hugely detrimental impact on the economy.

would find it difficult to get her Dominican ID. As her interactions with the Dominican Republic civil registry were fraught with problems, she decided to register as a Haitian. Rather than use her state-issued Dominican documentation, she borrowed a Haitian birth certificate from her neighbour and registered under a false name. To gain some clarity on this, I asked her:

> OK. So, you're telling me that you had a Dominican birth certificate, but because the [civil registry] had told you they didn't recognise the validity of this document, instead you decided the best course of action would be to register as a foreigner? You went to your friend and asked her to give you her [Haitian] birth certificate. You then took this document (knowing it didn't belong to you) and used it to register as a Haitian. Is that correct?

To which she replied, 'Yes.' We then both laughed at the absurdity of this situation. She reasoned that she was afraid because the authorities did not want to give her a Dominican identity card. She thought it would be best to register as a Haitian under another name. I asked her what she could have done with the 'Haitian' card. She responded, 'Nothing.'

After a concerted amount of effort and worry, the woman was eventually issued her new Dominican ID. I asked her what motivation she had for getting this document. She said, the police used to stop and ask for her papers. She hoped that this would not happen again. The next step, she told me, was to register her two children. Her Haitian partner already had problems at the health clinic when he took the children there. She said she had tried to register them before but thought that if her husband could not get the documents he needed then she would declare them children of a single Dominican woman. 'It would just be easier to take him out of the equation altogether,' she added.

This third case illustrates that although most persons in Group B were born to two Haitian parents, persons of Haitian ancestry were still treated with a form of permanent foreignness by the authorities. This meant that many were told to register as migrants even when their family had lived in the Dominican Republic over several generations. In this example, the woman's parents were born in the Dominican Republic, but because of difficulties in proving this, she was also caught up in the Group B registrations.

The woman told me that her Haitian grandparents were *de aquel lado* ('from over the border'), but her parents were born in the Dominican town of Barahona in the south-west of the country. She had five sons and three daughters, all of whom were undocumented. They worked in the coffee and sugar industry. Her father had a work permit but never declared his children. She was born at home and so had no way of accessing birth records.

The woman had heard about the new registrations from someone in her community. She went with her mother's birth certificate and declarations from seven witnesses who confirmed she was born in the country. She said that although her mother had been born in the Dominican Republic, she had been given a Haitian birth certificate in the town by embassy representatives. They charged people 200 pesos for the documents. She said that in her community it was far easier to get a Haitian birth certificate than a Dominican one, noting:

> They were giving them [Haitian birth certificates] out to anyone who wanted one.

The first time the informant attempted to get a Dominican birth certificate, a registry official in Monte Plata told her that the application was incomplete. She paid a lawyer 3,800 pesos – a substantial amount of money – to help her complete the process. The woman tried to deposit her documents on three different occasions. She said there were a lot of people waiting. She was eventually forced to register as a migrant through the PNRE because she could not see that she had any other choice. The woman had no documents to prove where she was born, and this made things very difficult, she told me.

She obtained her 'regularisation' card from the MIP, which confirmed her status as a Dominican-born Haitian. She asked what on earth she could do with a card that identified her as a foreigner. She did not understand why, as she was born in the country, she was registered as a Haitian. She also noted the number of Haitians and Dominicans waiting together for their papers. They talked about the process and asked each other what documents they needed and how the process worked. She told me that she did not want to be forced to stand in line for immigration because she was born here. She stated:

> I told someone [waiting for registrations] that I didn't want documents from immigration. What am I going to do with a document that's meant for foreigners? What am I going to do if I'm not allowed to get a *cédula*? I can't do anything with this document [she shows me her regularisation card]. About two months ago, I went to buy a phone and they didn't want to sell me one. They told me I couldn't get a SIM card because I wasn't registered [as a Dominican]. There are a lot of things I've wanted to do but can't. I can't get a good job with this card because they tell me I don't appear in the system. I'm not allowed to vote.

The informant said that she would like to go to the civil registry to try and get a Dominican ID once the card expired but did not really understand what she needed to do to get this.[15] She said she saw the registrations as a trick and that the government had no intention of ever giving people in Group B their documents. Nevertheless, she needed the new Dominican card to register her children, to work, to vote. Frustratingly for the woman, her husband had his Dominican ID. His status made no difference to her situation, she noted:

> A father cannot register his children. They tell him he can't do this on his own. A mother is allowed to do this, but a father can't. They [the civil registry] don't give out documents. They say no. My partner hasn't even bothered to do this. We haven't even tried as we know they'll just say no.

The woman told me that her new document was worthless and she did not even walk around with it in her purse. 'What's the point?' she said. It was a lot of effort to get, but no one ever asks her to produce it. She is regularly asked for her Dominican ID which she does not have. This has created problems. When she goes to the clinic for some tests, she cannot get these done, so usually she takes a neighbour's card instead. Nowadays, you even need an ID to work as a maid, she told me. The woman used to work in Herrera, an industrial town to the west of Santo Domingo, and in Sabana Larga, a rural town in the southwest of the country. She used to cook, clean and wash dishes for different families. Without a Dominican ID card, she has had to stop working as the recruitment agency she was registered with has now taken her off their books. She told me:

> For people like me, life is getting much more difficult.

Anglo-Descended (*Cocolo*) Populations

I decided to interview two Black Dominicans of Anglo-Caribbean heritage (known as *cocolos*) to compare and contrast their experiences with those of persons of Haitian ancestry who were overwhelmingly affected by the *Sentencia*. My interview with these two women, both in their late 70s, also provided some historical context into the registrations which they linked to their memories of the Trujillo dictatorship. They drew parallels between the new, biometric

---

15. Following the introduction of Law 169-14, the state promised that persons recorded within Group B as foreigners would then be able to apply for a Dominican identity card after a two-year period. There is little to no evidence that those within this group have successfully managed to (re)naturalise as Dominicans and obtain their original citizenship status.

ID card and their past experiences of increased state control and surveillance during this era.

The first woman was born in Santo Domingo. Her father, from Antigua, had died in an industrial accident when her mother was three months pregnant. She recounted how a woman called *Doña Marta* (Lady Marta) had travelled to Saint Kitts to recruit her mother and sent her to work on the island. Doña Marta, it transpired, was a mistress who would take young girls to the country to work as prostitutes. The woman told me about her difficult childhood. Her mother struggled as she did not speak Spanish and did not know a lot of people. She spoke about feeling very different to other people from a young age. She recounted how she used to play in Parque Julia Molina in Santo Domingo.[16] Children would jump out, pull her hair and call her *haitiana*, she said.

The second informant was born in San Pedro de Macorís in the east of the island. Her mother was from Antigua and her father from Anguilla. Her parents arrived in the country by boat as there were no planes at that time to transport people. The fathers of the informants originally arrived to cut sugar cane. She had been issued two ID cards in her life. The first, during the dictatorship. The second, with the recent registrations. She told me she had never experienced any problems in acquiring her documents. She nevertheless recalled how the military would threaten people in the street for mistakenly thinking that they were 'talking Haitian'. The informant told me how ashamed she was to speak English outside of the home for fear of mistreatment. She remembered how, in the 1940s and 1950s, people without identification were stopped and the police would often arrest them. The *cocolos*, she stated, were mistaken for Haitians because of their dark skin colour. She said she found it suspicious that the government was now so concerned with registering everybody especially now that ID cards had become so central to accessing specific services:

> You have to get the new ID [for everything]. If you don't have it, you are nothing. You need it. You can't do anything. In a hospital, an office, whatever happens you need your card.

The two women told me they had obtained the new card with relative ease. Nevertheless, a civil registry official in San Pedro de Macorís noted a misspelt name on the second woman's birth certificate. She thought it was too

---

16. This is now called Parque Enriquillo.

cumbersome to rectify the error and so kept the mistake on her new document. She told me she was not happy about this. Her name was important to her, she said.

Paradoxically, although the two informants had told me how they had once been the target of state oppression and discrimination, in recent years the situation for *cocolo*-descended populations had changed drastically. Since the economy began expanding and neoliberal reforms were introduced in the 1990s, there were new opportunities for the descendants of *cocolos*. This group had some grasp of English, a fact now celebrated rather than rejected as something foreign or suspicious. *Cocolo* descendants are sought after to work in tourism and FTZs. The poor, she noted, were having a difficult time and work was hard to come by. The *cocolos*, however, are now seen as useful to the economy and the state valued their presence. They are treated much better than they had been in the past. Our interview ended with her saying:

> It's not as bad as it used to be. At least they no longer think we're Haitians.

Other Persons of Non-Haitian Descent

Many of the registered populations of non-Haitian descent I spoke with complained much more about their interactions with the civil registry than persons of non-foreign lineage. They saw the civil registry as a nuisance and could not explain or understand why they were experiencing problems. Most did not link the changes they were experiencing to problems with 'Haitians' in the country. None were told directly by the civil registry that they had been included in Group A and some never realised this was why they were struggling to obtain their papers. This sometimes led to direct confrontations with civil registry officials. Here, I share the stories of two women included in Group A: one born to Japanese and the other to Argentinean parents.

The first woman I spoke with was a 44-year-old born in the rural village of Jima Abajo in La Vega to Japanese parents. They arrived in the country after World War II to work in rice production, which formed part of the foreign colonies encouraged by the Trujillo regime to bring their agricultural skills to the country. The informant told me how, at the time, Japan was mired in poverty and many were desperate to find work or travel abroad in search of a better life. She talked about how *la simpatía del tirano* ('the tyrant's charm') was a double-edged sword. She was fortunate, she said, that the dictator favoured the Japanese. He wanted them to modernise farming methods, and because they were not Haitians, he saw them as 'white' and therefore useful actors in his nation-building project.[17] The informant's mother arrived in the town of Dajabón on the Haitian-Dominican border at the age of 9 and her father in Constanza, in the central region, at the age of 14. Some of the immigrants they travelled with also settled in nearby Jarabacoa.

The woman told me that as the family did not grow up in a Japanese colony and her parents had arrived in the country at such a young age, they had a lot of influence of Dominican culture. They ate Dominican food. They also spoke Spanish at home although she later studied Japanese as an adult. The informant was registered at birth and got her first *cédula* when she was 16. She was thankful to her parents for doing that. She was aware that her name was in Group A but was surprised that this was the case especially as she thought she had all of her paperwork in order. Nevertheless, she did not see it as a big problem. She went straight to the JCE and had to answer some questions about her family, her neighbourhood and her personal life. The registry officials did not ask her for any more paperwork, and she got her new card relatively quickly. When I asked her what her *dominicanidad* meant to her, she said:

> *Dominicanidad* is a political term. It's like a form of blackmail. Some people use it as a shield, but I think it goes deeper than that. It's appropriation, responsibility and belonging. It's not just about going around waving a flag at a baseball match or a concert. It also means having an awareness about the problems in this country and trying to look for ways to solve them. I don't see any relationship between my documents and my identity. Nationality and identity are not the same thing. Identity is something that makes you concerned about what happens in your country. If something happens in Japan, that makes me sad but not as sad as when something happens here. Nationality is where you are born and the country that welcomes you. There are foreigners who get their paperwork because their family is living and working in a country. That doesn't mean their roots belong to that place.

The informant was very well travelled and had visited Japan, Brazil, Mexico, Paraguay, Peru and the United States. She said she always travels with her Japanese passport because of the hassle getting a visa for her Dominican

---

17. See the fantastic work of Yadira Perez Hazel for a fascinating insight into the experiences of Japanese-descended communities and how this relates to constructs of whiteness in the Dominican Republic. Y. Perez Hazel, 'Whiteness in Paradise: Japanese Immigrant Narratives of Identity, Collective Action, and Japan's National Responsibility', *Asian Ethnicity* 17, no. 3 (2016): 435–55.

passport. She told me she gets annoyed sometimes when people call her *china* ('Chinese'). She always corrects people and tells them that she is Dominican, but her parents are Japanese. She added:

> My roots belong in the Dominican Republic. It's my country [...] even when Dominicans don't see me as Dominican and in Japan they don't see me as Japanese.

This final example underlines some of the problems persons of non-Haitian ancestry born to two non-Dominican parents have experienced with legal identity measures. This informant was a white woman born in the sugar-producing town of La Romana to Argentinean parents. Her parents arrived in the Dominican Republic via the United States during the Argentinean dictatorship. They were not permanent residents and registered her birth using a work visa as opposed to the (now required) Dominican ID card.[18] The woman said that she identified strongly with Dominican culture. She sang the national anthem every day at school and felt a close bond to the country. She was a social activist who cared about where she was from. She was, she noted, a 'good and active citizen'. She had participated in marches and always tried to vote.

In 2008, the woman needed a copy of her birth certificate to register with the Ministry of Education for the national exams. This, she told me, was the first time she discovered there was a serious problem with her recorded status. She tried to resolve the issue with the civil registry in Santo Domingo but was sent back to La Romana. Staff there did not explain why they were refusing to issue her a copy of her birth certificate. She subsequently sought help from a family friend who was a lawyer. The woman expressed confusion with the situation, noting that the civil registry official who refused to give her a copy of her papers was the very same person who had signed her original Dominican birth certificate.[19] To her, this was a ludicrous situation. It made no sense to her why suddenly this government official could treat her so differently to others waiting in line.

In contrast to the informants of Haitian descent I met with, this woman was unaware of her Group A status. Instead, she saw her problems as an example of greater state surveillance in the country. In 2013, she had participated in an

---

18. I was not shown a copy of these visas, so cannot verify whether this information is entirely correct.

19. In other words, due to her Argentinean ancestry, she did not automatically link the actions of the civil registry to legal identity measures affecting Haitian-descended populations. She therefore interpreted the situation as illogical.

anti-corruption protest. The following day, a registry official phoned her house to discuss her case. She said she got really upset about the situation. She felt singled out because she was queried about the validity of her national status. She saw this as a sign that the government was creating a database of political activists and was using this information to threaten people. The situation made her feel scared and unsafe.

Initially, the woman had not been overly concerned about the problems she was facing, but gradually she began to see her treatment as unjust and discriminatory. She grew more and more upset. She could also see how angry the situation made her father and that this was creating a conflict within the family. She said that the civil registry officials talked about her nationality a lot. They told her the state did not recognise her as a Dominican. She could not understand how this could happen. Her mother had already naturalised as a Dominican and had always had her paperwork. She had spent her whole life in the Dominican Republic but was regularly told she was not from there.

When she went to the Argentinean embassy, they said she could not register there either. Effectively, this rendered her stateless. The situation bothered her a lot. She said it made her feel like an alien from outer space, like she did not belong on this planet. She acknowledged that she was not always accepted and that as a white woman she doesn't typically 'look' Dominican. She thought that for some she would never really be accepted as a Dominican because she was white. This bothered her, she told me.

In January 2015, the woman was granted an interview at the civil registry in Santo Domingo to verify her status. She took her old ID and all the documents she had. She had represented the country in international competitions and took the certificates for those with her too. During the interview process, a state official asked her basic questions about her life: where she was from, where she went to school, the names of her neighbours, her nicknames as a child. She said they did this to test her and see if she had lived her whole life in the country and if she identified with the Dominican culture. The woman said it was not a difficult process and many of the questions did not have a right or wrong answer. She was, however, tired of navigating bureaucratic hurdles and wanted to find a way out of her predicament, stating:

At that point, I decided to play the part of a smart little good girl. My mum sent me to get my hair done, she made me take out my earrings. I dressed well. I wanted to look calm. I said, 'Oh, look how lucky we are! We have found out about this and now we can come and resolve this issue.' But in reality, on the inside, I was really angry. I didn't understand how, out of nowhere, a person could lose their nationality and no-one tells you. That's what happened to me in 2008. No one told me anything. Nothing at all.

The woman told me she did not have to wait a long time and the process was over relatively quickly. After years of frustration, she was able to obtain her new biometric card. While at the civil registry, she was told that the system had flagged up a problem with her sister's file.[20] Because her sister was still a minor, the official worked on their two cases and asked that she answer questions on behalf of her sibling. When this interview ended, her sister also obtained her new ID. The informant's anger was nevertheless palpable. She was furious that the state could query the legitimacy of her Dominican identity. Not only was she expected to be thankful to the state for resolving her issues, but now had to demonstrate a form of docility to exist within it. This concerned her immensely:

A person is not just their nationality. *Dominicanidad* is a word that limits you, it restricts you to a certain role. It is not just about beer, the *malecón* (seafront), the beach or drinking rum. It is a word that we are using to organise people.

The interview process for this white woman was straightforward, but the years of problems she had faced had worn her down. She said she was frustrated but decided not to fight the system any longer. The experience had made her see her Dominican identity from a new perspective, she told me.

Concluding Thoughts

The aim of this chapter was to amplify the voices of Dominican citizens from varying socioeconomic backgrounds and national and ethnic origins to underline their multifaceted experiences of legal identity measures. I have demonstrated how individuals have had to learn to (re)negotiate their interactions with state officials and circumnavigate state architectures to (re)obtain the legal identity documentation that, regrettably, was rightfully theirs from the outset. By focusing largely on the experiences of un-Dominicans – persons who have struggled in some capacity to gain or retain their recognition as citizens – I have shown how international policy that promulgates universal legal identity has had a discriminatory and negative impact on Haitian-descended populations, individuals of non-Haitian ancestry as well

---

20. I verified this information and found that the sister of the informant had also been named in Group A. All data relating to this file has been kept confidential.

as Black Dominicans of no immediate foreign ancestry specifically because of their race, non-Dominican or ethnic origin.

By linking global contemporary identification and legal identity measures with the lived experiences of Dominican citizens, I have highlighted how efforts to bureaucratically (re)categorise individuals as non-nationals have kept people within their socioeconomic space, detaching them from associated citizenship privileges. Despite the importance international organisations are now placing on the need for documentation and their efforts to promote the positive stories of individuals who have benefitted from registrations, the theme of apathy as well as weariness was evident with many people who participated in the interviews for this book. For the income-poor, these measures were overly cumbersome particularly as the most basic of administrative tasks encompassed additional costs, such as transport and food, yet were necessary so that they could access healthcare and benefits for their children and families. All informants understood the practical value of their ID and recognised the limitations for people who did not have their paperwork. They knew an ID card gave them access to different spaces, opportunities and experiences, while those unable to acquire documentation were struggling. One informant noted the irony of the situation, stating:

> It's [a Dominican ID/passport] not really that great, is it? Dominicans need a visa to go practically anywhere. In the broader scheme of things, it's really not the most useful of documents.

In contrast to the claims of NGOs and human rights organisations who place overwhelming importance on the emotional attachment populations have to their ID, many informants did not see their papers as a vehicle to accessing or unlocking rights, simply as something the state demanded while they reluctantly complied. It was clear that although there had been a huge impetus to provide Dominicans with their new biometric card and a high level of investment in state architectures and legal identity measures, some people still cared very little about documentation. In poorer communities, many did not have a strong affinity to their paperwork. They did see their ID as a badge of their identity, but they were not overly concerned with whether their card classified them as Dominican, Haitian or other. Instead, they knew they needed their ID to get on in life. And for those unable to overcome their documentation woes, life was becoming much, much more difficult.

Chapter 6

TOWARDS A DIGITAL ERA: CLOSING THE GLOBAL IDENTITY GAP

Refugiado ciudadano de ningún lado
Libre pero esclavo
Viajero, no importa donde vaya
Siempre seré extranjero.

[A refugee, citizen from nowhere
Free but still a slave
It doesn't matter where I go or travel
I'll always be a foreigner].[1]

The Dominican Republic is the leading country of origin of unauthorised migrants from the Caribbean.[2] Close to 2 million Dominicans – approximately one-fifth of the entire population – and their descendants are now thought to live in the United States. This constitutes the fifth largest Latino group in the United States with most migrants settling in New York or Miami.[3] While a limited number of Dominicans and Haitians arrive via boat under highly perilous circumstances, the majority land in the United States with a

---

1. Lyrics: Dios Salve al Viajero, by the Dominican rock band Toque Profundo, 1993.
2. The Immigrant Visa Unit of the US embassy in Santo Domingo is one of the largest diplomatic missions in the world. After Mexico (89,234 Mexicans, 14.5 per cent of total issuances), the Dominican Republic is the second largest country to issue immigrant visas, with 53,339 Dominicans receiving travel documentation in 2016, 8.6 per cent of total issuances worldwide. See US Department of State, Bureau of Consular Affairs, 'Immigrant Visas Issued at Foreign Service Posts by Country of Birth/Chargeability Fiscal Year 2016'; A. Brown and E. Patten, *Hispanics of Dominican Origin in the United States*, 2013, http://www.pewhispanic.org/2013/06/19/hispanics-of-dominican-origin-in-theunited-states-2011/..
3. P. Guadalupe, *As Their Numbers Grow, Dominican-Americans Solidify Their Presence and Clout*, 2018. NBC News. Original article: https://www.nbcnews.com/news/latino/their-numbers-grow-dominican-americans-solidify-their-presence-clout-n851386

commercial airline having acquired a passport and tourist visa. A proportion of these migrants eventually become illegal over-stayers when their documents expire and they are then forced to remain – undetected – in the country.

Until recently, the undocumented status of Dominicans living overseas meant that many were hesitant or unable to renew their passport. This made it impossible for thousands of Dominicans to resolve their irregular status with the US authorities. The overhaul of the country's social policy sector, the expansion of new digital technologies and the modernisation of the civil registry have ensured that transnational Dominican populations can now access their legal identity documentation from anywhere in the world with diplomatic representation. As migrants, they no longer have to make the long and expensive journey back to their place of birth to acquire their documents. These changes have transformed the lives of millions of Dominicans and their descendants living overseas as they can now obtain their national identity card, renew their passport and vote without ever having to step foot on the island.

One woman I interviewed for this book gave a chilling account of the dangers Dominicans and Haitians face if they decide to leave in search of a better life. Born in the Bay of Samaná, a coastal town in the north-east of the country, she recounted that as a child she was regularly awoken in the middle of the night by the screams of people drowning in the ocean desperate to get to Puerto Rico by boat. Many who managed to reach the neighbouring island did so in the hope that they could use it as a springboard to one day arrive on the US mainland. The woman was married to a Haitian man, a pastor, who had migrated to the Dominican Republic. She had heard warnings in the media that the new identity card would be compulsory and people who did not update their documents were likely to encounter problems. She said that although both countries faced hardships and people struggled to make ends meet, no matter how precarious or difficult life was for Dominicans, the one single item of value they possessed over Haitian migrants was their ID document as citizens. The card gave them a superior status over their neighbours. They could then use it to work and provide for their family. She told me:

> Dominicans dream of going to a bigger 'country' like Puerto Rico. Haiti was terrible. I went before the earthquake. They have a lot of beautiful places, but it is much worse there. It's like two different worlds. The world of the rich who live like they are in Hollywood and the life of the [everyday] people. We compare ourselves to what is better, not worse. […] Poor Dominicans are at the bottom of the ladder, but Haitians will always be lower. A Dominican thinks he is superior to Haitians. His documentation is like a badge of honour, a gift from the state.

Legal identity was never really about guaranteeing the legal recognition of Dominicans. Instead, registration drives helped the authorities implement the new biometric card as an exclusionary tool to block Haitian-descended populations from accessing their Dominican ID documents and truncating their opportunities along the way. While eager to take the World Bank's lead in promoting a legal identity for all – not least to continue benefitting from external funding and support – the state balked at pressure to recognise persons born to Haitian migrants as Dominican citizens no matter how old they were or over how many generations they had lived in the country.

We have seen in this book that the large-scale identification of citizens, promoted widely by international development organisations, big tech companies and the banking sector not only targeted undocumented, informal and stateless populations but also has the potential to affect all of us. As international actors promote legal and, increasingly, digital identity as a vehicle for inclusion, this book has illustrated that we need to think more closely about how states can implement these systems as a form of racial (re)ordering, surveillance and discrimination. Rather than see legal identity for all as the ultimate goal, practitioners must instead approach the SDGs from a position of pragmatism. As the statelessness expert Laura van Waas rightly acknowledges:

> Neither legal identity nor nationality is really the end game, it's about what flows from them, i.e. a greater equality, greater inclusion and greater ability to claim rights.[4]

At the start of this book, I argued that the Dominican case provides us with a cautionary tale about the potential disputes that can arise over who should have access to a legal identity. As discussed in Chapter 1, legal identity – the provision of a birth certificate to everyone, everywhere – is now a core component of global policy. Despite its central role in the international development sector, empirical analysis of the impact on the 'users' of these systems – that is, citizens - has been notably absent from contemporary debates on citizenship, noncitizenship and statelessness. I observe how, in the international development sector, debates on identification measures, and the technologies that support them, are typically couched within a discourse of belonging, social inclusion and the universal right to a legal identity. I underline that history has already shown us we should expect to encounter problems with ID systems and the allocation of birth certificates is inevitably interconnected with broader

---

4. L. van Waas, *The Right to a Legal Identity or the Right to a Legal ID?* European Network on Statelessness, 2015, https://www.statelessness.eu/blog/right-legal-identity-or-right-legal-id..

registrations, such as the national ID card and passport. Although SDG 16.9 is doing very well in achieving the universal registration of children, I highlight that contestations over which populations should have/retain access to a legal identity are erupting around the world. This is especially concerning for migrant-descended adult populations born in a country yet not accepted as a member of the body politic. This book therefore provides a timely example of the limitations of legal identity practices particularly when targeted at Afro-descended and Indigenous populations.

In Chapter 2, I note that Hispaniola lay at the very centre of the global slave trade which was administered via a colonial system that purposely excluded Indigenous peoples, the poor, women and the Afro-descended from formal recognition as citizens. I argue that race on the island has been consistently (re)imagined, hierarchically structured and/or (mis)used for political and economic gain. Colonial regimes relied on complex caste systems, racial categorisations and *blanqueamiento* (the process of whitening the race) to dominate, enslave and control populations. Contemporary debates on ID systems must acknowledge this troublesome past of white supremacy, slavery, forced labour and racial exclusion. Highlighting the 'permanent foreignness' of Haitian-descended populations, the chapter shows how the authorities refused to recognise people born to Haitian migrants as Dominican citizens. Until this book, studies have tended to focus on the experiences of Haitian migrants together with those of their Dominican-born children in areas where cases of statelessness are prevalent: the *batey* and the Haitian-Dominican border. I argue, however, that in order to understand the diverse, heterogenous and complex make-up of the Dominican people, we need to also consider the experiences of people living beyond these places. Rather than assume that anti-Haitian nationalist prejudice is sufficient enough an explanation for the foreign-making actions of the Dominican state, we must *dehaitianise* our approaches to this case. As I have stated, this is by no means to diminish or detract attention from the outrageous mistreatment Haitian migrants and their descendants have suffered at the hands of the Dominican authorities. Instead, it is to highlight how ID systems can be used to cast doubt and challenge belonging over who are citizens and who are foreigners. This will help us look to broader, more global explanations regarding the implementation of en masse registrations and their potential for exclusion.

In Chapter 3, I showed how access to social protection is intrinsically tied to providing cash transfer payments to beneficiaries with a valid ID document. The decision as to which individuals are identified as citizens eligible for welfare payments rests firmly with the state. I highlighted the role of international actors, such as the World Bank, Inter-American Development Bank and the United Nations, in pushing the state to provide Dominicans with ID to ensure the uptake of social welfare programmes. I show how this resulted in a complete overhaul of the social policy sector which specifically designed state architectures that would share information from the civil registry with government departments responsible for welfare payments and healthcare provision, among others, with the aim of intentionally blocking the Haitian-descended from obtaining or renewing their Dominican ID.

Tensions over who should be recognised as Dominican citizens culminated in the 2013 *Sentencia* we examine in Chapter 4 which stripped the plaintiff Juliana Deguis Pierre of her Dominican nationality, rendering her stateless. I have shown how this landmark ruling, which was met with widespread condemnation and outrage, caused the largest statelessness crisis in the Americas. It resulted in the creation of a national audit that publicly named and shamed tens of thousands of persons whose citizenship was now in doubt, a large majority of whom were born to Haitian migrants. Within this process, some formerly documented Dominicans were able to renew their paperwork and therefore retain their citizenship status (Group 'A'). Others were told to present themselves to the authorities and register as foreigners with the promise that they could later (re)'naturalise' as citizens (Group 'B'). The registrations led to chaotic scenes which gave civil registry officials a space to challenge and refute the legitimacy of people's claim to a Dominican nationality.

Chapter 5 amplified the voices of un-Dominicans – people who at one point were recognised in law as citizens yet have had to overcome significant administrative and bureaucratic obstacles to (re)obtain their legal identity as Dominicans. Through a focus on (largely) migrant-descended populations, I have highlighted the impact of large-scale international identification measures on individual experiences of legal identity. I have shown how changes to the Dominican civil registry were especially worrying for Black populations who did not fit comfortably within the state's vision of national identity and entitlement. In an attempt to purge any association with Haitians from the body politic, the state utilised external donor-sponsored registrations to (re)envision and (re)mould its own version of *dominicanidad*.

We heard from a Black woman of no immediate foreign ancestry who was denied a birth certificate for her son because a civil registry official decided that she 'looked Haitian'. We saw how in the same family three brothers born to Haitian parents had wildly different interactions with the state. The first man was forced by a civil registry official to cut off his Afro hair before renewing his card, suffering repeated racial harassment and incarceration at the hands of the police; the second got his ID with no real effort; the third man never managed to get his documents at all and instead was told to register as a Haitian.

In addition, we heard how a Black man living overseas was paraded around as a Dominican by government officials at meetings and diplomatic gatherings in an attempt not to appear anti-Haitian or racist. Behind the scenes, however, this man found himself in a dispute with an embassy official who was refusing to renew his Dominican passport because he was born to Haitian parents. We also saw how registrations after the *Sentencia* as part of Law 169-14 created confusion and upset as one woman mistakenly registered first as a Haitian via Group B then as a Dominican via Group A because she was frightened and did not understand how to navigate these processes.

In the final interview, a social activist born to Argentinean parents was caught up in the post-*Sentencia* fallout and left stateless. After a long battle with the authorities, she eventually managed to obtain her legal identity but was very aware that her race and social standing had given her an advantage over Haitian-descended Dominicans still struggling for state recognition. These examples show how practices that centralise the provision of state and banking services through an ID form part of a much broader destabilising process that not only affects children born to Haitians but are also interconnected with one another. Far from expulsing the Haitian-descended to a country many had never been to, instead the state aimed to utilise state architectures and the new biometric national identity card to keep populations in situ, creating perpetual domestic 'foreigners'. These measures had an impact on individuals across different socioeconomic backgrounds, living both domestically and overseas, and far beyond the populations they initially intended to target. This has led to:

> opportunities to escape from poverty being systematically walled off. Not by barbed wire fences or guards toting firearms but by identity documents, computerised databases and institutional gatekeepers.[5]

In June 2021, I organised the two-day conference '(Re)Imagining Belonging in Latin America and Beyond: Access to Citizenship, Digital Identity and Rights' with the Centre for Latin American and Caribbean Studies (CLACS), University of London. The event, organised in collaboration with the Institute on Statelessness and Inclusion, explored the intersections between legal identity and perceptions of belonging, the growing importance of digital ID in international development and the impact of global identification practices on citizenship rights. The themes presented at this conference were far-reaching and innovative. They included challenges to legal definitions of status, particularly for migrant-descended and non-binary people; a sociohistorical examination of nation-building practices across the Americas; analysis of the recent

---

5. S. Martínez, 'Anti-Haitian Exclusionism in the Dominican Republic', YouTube video, Center for Religion, Ethics and Culture, 2015.

Windrush scandal in the United Kingdom; an exploration of citizenship-stripping, statelessness and foreign-making practices in the region;[6] and the impact of biometrics on the fundamental rights of the citizen; among others. From these conversations, it became very clear that the Dominican Republic is far from an anomaly in the region. Worryingly, if anything, the country is a trailblazer.

When completing the final edits for this book, the coronavirus struck. Challenges over how citizens are identified, who is deemed eligible for inclusion onto ID systems and which groups should be given access to life-saving vaccines will inevitably lead to increased tensions in responses to the pandemic. We need to consider how states are using vaccination passports, biometric ID cards and data-sharing track-and-trace systems to monitor, identify and classify populations. More so than ever, greater scrutiny is needed over who are we including and who is being left out of this digital revolution.

In the build-up to the 2030 SDGs, multilateral organisations are encouraging states to improve the bureaucratic procedures that mark the income-poor and ensure they are more easily identifiable to states, aid agencies and the banking sector. It is time we have a serious conversation about the interconnectedness of these practices with national ID programmes and their impact on the lived experiences of individuals. Debates are only going to become more prevalent over the next 10 years as states move towards the demand that all populations – migrant-descended and otherwise – are provided with legal proof of state membership.

For legal identity to be effective, more needs to be done to critically assess the ways in which this target might be counterproductive to the overall aims of the SDGs as it has the potential to (re)produce inequality, exacerbate statelessness and contribute to exclusion. The findings in this book therefore challenge the implicit normativity of international development policy that assumes the universal provision of legal identity inclusionary for all. These observations are of global import and offer some worrying insights into the use of modern-day identification systems for authoritarian purposes.

---

6. For example, Cuba and the United States are two countries with cases of stateless populations.

GLOSSARY OF DOMINICAN TERMS AND PHRASES

acta	a birth certificate
amancebado	a (typically unmarried) couple that is living together/cohabiting
antihaitianismo	a term used to describe discrimination towards and hatred of Haitians in the Dominican Republic
aplatana'o	a foreigner who has culturally assimilated as a Dominican (meaning to turn into a *plátano*, i.e. plantain)
barrido	a 'sweep': a term used to describe the *en masse* collation of data from households across the length and breadth of the country
batey(es)	enclosed rural sugar plantations (largely privatised since the 1970s) where Haitian migrants and their descendants have lived and formed communities in the Dominican Republic
buscones	tricksters who try and obtain money in exchange for documentation
canasta básica	basic essential food items necessary to feed the average Dominican household
cédula de identidad y electoral	the Dominican national identity card
cédula de menor	an identity card issued to young mothers who are under the age of 18 so they can register their child
cocolos	Afro-descended populations in the Dominican Republic with roots in the Anglophone, Francophone and Dutch Caribbean
colmado	Dominican grocery stores selling basic food items; *colmados* are often the centre of both rural and urban communities and the main locations for the disbursement of cash transfer payments to welfare beneficiaries

Comer es Primero	Dominican targeted cash transfer (CT) programme for populations living in extreme poverty
Constancia de Nacido Vivo	hospital record of the birth of a child in public health facilities
(el) dao	used to explain the state culture of gift-giving to the poor for political support
del otro lado	a phrase Dominicans use to describe people 'from the other side' of the island, i.e. Haitians
Dominicanos y Dominicanas con Nombre y Apellido	the registration initiative entitled Dominicans with a first and last name
dominicanidad	the state of being a Dominican; regularly, however, the term is also used to emphasise an imagined 'white', Catholic, Hispanic identity over one that is Black, Haitian and African
ficha	work permit
(la) fundita	used to explain the state culture of gift-giving to the poor for political support
haitiano	the term 'Haitian' is regularly used to identify Haitian-descended populations, even when born in the country over several generations and in possession of state-issued Dominican paperwork
haitiano de aquí	Haitian from here, a term commonly used to talk about Haitian-descended populations born in the Dominican Republic
indio	a focus on the (largely imagined) indigeneity of the Dominican people allowed for a racial category that was neither Black nor white
kreyòl	Haitian Creole
la Sentencia	Constitutional Tribunal decision 168–13
levantamiento	the collation of data for a survey
Libro de Extranjería	Registry of Foreigners
machetero	person holding a machete, such as a plantation worker
Programa Solidaridad	Dominican cash transfer and welfare benefits initiative
tollo	from *atolladero*, meaning a bureaucratic mess or general disorder
transeúnte	non-resident, a transient person

BIBLIOGRAPHY

Abel, C., and Lewis, C. M. (eds) (2015) *Latin America, Economic Imperialism and the State: The Political Economy of the External Connection from Independence to the Present, Latin America, Economic Imperialism and the State*. London: Bloomsbury Academic.

Aber, S., and Small, M. (2013) 'Citizen or Subordinate: Permutations of Belonging in the United States and the Dominican Republic', *Journal on Migration and Human Security*, 1(3), pp. 76–96.

Achiume, E. T. (2020) *Report of the Special Rapporteur on Contemporary Forms of Racism, Racial Discrimination, Xenophobia and Related Intolerance*. New York: United Nations.

Agamben, G. (1995) *Homo Sacer: Sovereign Power and Bare Life*. Redwood City, CA: Stanford University Press.

Agarwal, M., and Sengupta, D. (1999) 'Structural Adjustment in Latin America: Policies and Performance', *Economic and Political Weekly*, 34(44), pp. 3129–36.

Ajana, B. (2012) 'Biometric Citizenship', *Citizenship Studies*, 16(7), pp. 851–70.

——— (2013) *Governing through Biometrics: The Biopolitics of Identity*. London: Palgrave Macmillan.

Anderson, B. (1983) *Imagined Communities: Reflections on the Origin and Spread of Nationalism*. London: Verso.

Apland, K., Hamilton, C., Blitz, B. K., Lagaay, M., Lakshman, R., and Yarrow, E. (2015) *Birth Registration and Children's Rights: A Complex Story*. Report of Coram Children's Legal Centre, Woking, England. Available at: https://www.planusa.org/docs/reports/2014-birth-registration-research-full-report.pdf.

Asamblea Nacional (2010) *Constitución de la República Dominicana de 2010*.

Balaguer, J. (1985) *La Isla Al Revés: Haití y el Destino Dominicano*. Santo Domingo: Libreria Dominicana.

Bartlett, L., Jayaram, K., and Bonhomme, G. (2011) 'State Literacies and Inequality: Managing Haitian Immigrants in the Dominican Republic', *International Journal of Educational Development*, 31(6), pp. 587–95.

Belton, K. A. (2015) 'Rooted Displacement: The Paradox of Belonging among Stateless People', *Citizenship Studies*, 19(8), pp. 907–21.

Bhabha, J. (2009) 'Arendt's Children: Do Today's Migrant Children Have a Right to Have Rights?', *Human Rights Quarterly*, 31(2), pp. 410–51. doi:10.1353/hrq.0.0072.

Bhabha, J., and Robinson, M. (eds) (2011) *Children without a State: A Global Human Rights Challenge*. Cambridge: MIT Press.

Blake, J. (2014) 'Haiti, the Dominican Republic, and Race-Based Statelessness in the Americas', *Georgetown Journal of Law & Modern Critical Race Perspectives*, 6(2), pp. 139–80.

Bolívar Díaz, J. (2013) *El Constitucional ignora la Corte Interamericana*. Available at: http://hoy.com.do/el-constitucional-ignora-la-corte-interamericana/.

Brinham, N. (2019) 'Looking beyond Invisibility: Rohingyas' Dangerous Encounters with Papers and Cards', *Tilburg Law Review*, 24(2), pp. 156–69.

Britto, T. (2005) *Recent Trends in the Development Agenda of Latin America: An Analysis of Conditional Cash Transfers*. Manchester: Institute for Development Policy and Management.

Brown, A., and Patten, E. (2013) *Hispanics of Dominican Origin in the United States*. Available at: http://www.pewhispanic.org/2013/06/19/hispanics-of-dominican-origin-in-theunited-states-2011/.

Cambeira, A. (1997) *Quisqueya la Bella: Dominican Republic in Historical and Cultural Perspective*. New York: M. E. Sharpe.

Candelario, G. E. B. (2000) *Situating Ambiguity: Dominican Identity Formations*. New York: City University of New York.

Carrasco, H., Sandro Parodi, E. G., and Vásquez, M. (2016) *¿Cómo se redistribuyen los recursos públicos en República Dominicana?* Washington, DC: Banco Interamericano de Desarrollo.

Castillo Pantaleón, J. M. (2012) *La Nacionalidad Dominicana*. Santo Domingo: Editora Nacional.

Centro para la Observación Migratoria y el Desarrollo Social en el Caribe (OBMICA) (2018) *Facilitando el acceso al registro civil dominicano a descendientes de parejas mixtas: protocolo para su acompañamiento legal*. Santo Domingo: Editora Búho.

Chamberlain, M. (ed.) (1998) *Caribbean Migration: Globalized Identities*. Oxfordshire: Routledge.

Chandy, L. (2018) 'Since the Year 2000, over 130 Countries Have Started Digital ID Programs – Surely One of the Most Under-appreciated Revolutions in International Development', Twitter. Available at: https://twitter.com/laurencechandy/status/953453745416953856.

Civolani Hischnjakow, K. (2011) *Vidas Suspendidas: Efectos de la Resolución 012-07 en la población*. Santo Domingo: Centro Bonó. Revista Estudios Sociales. 41(154).

Cody, C. (2009) *Count Every Child: The Right to Birth Registration*. Woking, England: Plan International. Available at: http://plancanada.ca/downloads/CountEveryChildReport.pdf.

Congreso Nacional de la República Dominicana (2004) *Ley 285 sobre migración*. Santo Domingo: Gobierno Dominicano.

Crassweller, R. D. (1966) *Trujillo: The Life and Times of a Caribbean Dictator*. New York: Macmillan.

Cruz-Martínez, G. (2019) 'Rethinking Universalism: Older-Age International Migrants and Social Pensions in Latin American and the Caribbean', *Global Social Policy*, 20(1). doi:10.1177/1468018119873267.

Derby, L. H. (2009) *The Dictator's Seduction: Politics and the Popular Imagination in the Era of Trujillo*. Durham, NC: Duke University Press.

Dunning, C., Gelb, A., and Raghavan, S. (2014) 'Birth Registration, Legal Identity, and the Post-2015 Agenda', Center for Global Development, CGD Policy, September. Available at: http://www.cgdev.org/sites/default/files/birth-registration-legal-identity.pdf.

——— (2006) *The Under-Registration of Births in Latin America*. Washington, DC: Inter-American Development Bank.

Economic Commission for Latin America and the Caribbean (2010) *Time for Equality: Closing Gaps, Opening Trails*. Brasilia: ECLAC.

Eller, A. (2016) *We Dream Together: Dominican Independence, Haiti, and the Fight for Caribbean Freedom*. Durham, NC: Duke University Press.

Fanon, F. (1952) *Peau noir, masque blancs*. Paris: Éditions du Seuil.

Fariello, F., Boisson de Chazournes, L., and Davis, K. E. (eds) (2016) *The World Bank Legal Review. Financing and Implementing the Post-2015 Development Agenda: The Role of Law and Justice Systems. Volume 7.* Washington, DC: International Bank for Reconstruction and Development/World Bank.

Ferguson, J. (2003) 'Migration in the Caribbean: Haiti, the Dominican Republic and beyond', Report of Minority Rights Group International, pp. 2–38.

Fisher, A. B., and O'Hara, M. D. (eds) (2009) *Imperial Subjects: Race and Identity in Colonial Latin America.* Durham, NC: Duke University Press.

Fiszbein, A., and Schady, N. R. (2009) *Conditional Cash Transfers: Reducing Present and Future Poverty, World Bank Policy Report.* Washington, DC: World Bank.

Foster, M., and Roberts, J. (2021) 'Manufacturing Foreigners: The Law and Politics of Transforming Citizens into Migrants', in Catherine Dauvergne (ed.) *Research Handbook on the Law and Politics of Migration*, pp. 218–34. Northampton, MA: Elgar Publishing.

Fussell, J. (2001) 'Group Classification on National ID Cards as a Factor in Genocide and Ethnic Cleansing, Human Rights', Report presented to the Seminar Series of the Yale University Genocide Studies Program, Prevent Genocide International. http://www.preventgenocide.org/prevent/removing-facilitating-factors/IDcards/.

Gamboa, L., and Harrington Reddy, J. (2014) 'Judicial Denationalisation of Dominicans of Haitian Descent', *Forced Migration Review* 46.

Garay, C. (2016) *Social Policy Expansion in Latin America.* New York: Cambridge University Press.

García-Peña, L. (2016) *The Borders of Dominicanidad: Race, Nation and the Archives of Contradiction.* Durham, NC: Duke University Press.

Gelb, A., and Clark, J. (2013) 'Identification for Development: The Biometrics Revolution', Working paper 315, Center for Global Development, January), pp. 1–81.

de Genova, N. (2018a) 'Rebordering "the People": Notes on Theorizing Populism', *South Atlantic Quarterly*, 117(2), pp. 357–74.

———— (2018b) 'The Deportation Power', *Radical Philosophy*, 2.03 (December), pp. 23–27.

Giovanni, A. C., Jolly, R., and Stewart, F. (1987) *Adjustment with a Human Face: Protecting the Vulnerable and Promoting Growth. A Study by UNICEF.* 1st and 2nd ed. Oxford: Oxford University Press.

Goldring, L., and Landolt, P. (2013) *Producing and Negotiating Non-Citizenship: Precarious Legal Status in Canada.* Toronto: University of Toronto Press.

Gómez Nadal, P. (2017) *Indios, negros y otros indeseables. Capitalismo, racismo y exclusión en América Latina y el Caribe.* Quito: Fundación Rosa Luxemburg.

Guadalupe, P. (2018) 'As Their Numbers Grow, Dominican-Americans Solidify Their Presence and Clout', NBC News. Available at: https://www.nbcnews.com/news/latino/their-numbers-grow-dominican-americans-solidify-their-presence-clout-n851386.

Haiti Support Group (2014) 'Stateless in the Caribbean', *Haiti Briefing* 76.

Harbitz, M., and Boekle-Giuffrida, B. (2009) 'Democratic Governance, Citizenship, and Legal Identity: Linking Theoretical Discussion and Operational Reality', Inter-American Development Bank, Working Paper.

Harbitz, M., and del Carmen Tamargo, M. (2009) *The Significance of Legal Identity in Situations of Poverty and Social Exclusion: The Link between Gender, Ethnicity, and Legal Identity, Technical Note.* Washington, DC: IADB.

Hayes de Kalaf, E. (2010) 'Electricidad y Equidad en la República Dominicana: Una Perspectiva del Desarrollo Humano', Report, Santo Domingo.

———— (2015a) 'Dominican Republic Has Taken Citizenship from up to 200,000 and Is Getting Away with It, the Conversation'. Available at: https://theconversation.com/dominican-republic-has-taken-citizenship-from-up-to-200-000-and-is-getting-away-with-it-43161.

———— (2015b) 'How a Group of Dominicans Were Stripped of Their Nationality and Now Face Expulsion to Haiti, the Conversation'. Available at: https://theconversation.com/how-a-group-of-dominicans-were-stripped-of-their-nationality-and-now-face-expulsion-to-haiti-39658.

———— (2018) 'Making Foreign: Legal Identity, Social Policy and the Contours of Belonging in the Contemporary Dominican Republic', doctoral thesis, British Library EThOS.

———— (2019) 'Making Foreign: Legal Identity, Social Policy and the Contours of Belonging in the Contemporary Dominican Republic', in Cruz-Martínez, G. (ed.) *Welfare and Social Protection in Contemporary Latin America*, p. 102. London: Routledge.

Hindess, B. (2002) 'Neo-liberal Citizenship', *Citizenship Studies*, 6(2), pp. 127–43.

Hintzen, A. (2016) *Cultivating Resistance: Haitian-Dominican Communities and the Dominican Sugar Industry, 1915–1990*. Coral Gabes, FL: University of Miami.

Hosein, G., and Nyst, C. (2013) 'Aiding Surveillance', Privacy International. Available at: https://privacyinternational.org/report/841/aiding-surveillance.

Howard, D. (2001) *Coloring the Nation: Race and Ethnicity in the Dominican Republic*. Boulder, CO: Lynne Rienner.

———— (2017) 'Race and Modernity in Hispaniola: Tropical Matters and Development Perspectives', in Sansavior, E., and Scholar, R. (eds) *Caribbean Globalizations: From 1492 to the Present Day*, pp. 203–26. Liverpool: Liverpool University Press.

Huber, E., and Stephens, J. D. (2012) *Democracy and the Left: Social Policy and Inequality in Latin America*. Chicago: University of Chicago Press.

Human Rights Watch (2015) *We Are Dominican: Arbitrary Deprivation of Nationality in the Dominican Republic*. New York: Human Rights Watch.

Hunter, W. (2019) chapter 4, in Cammett, M., and Schneider, B. R. (eds) *Undocumented Nationals: Between Statelessness and Citizenship*, 37–52. Cambridge: Cambridge University Press.

Hunter, W., and Brill, R. (2016) ' "Documents, Please": Advances in Social Protection and Birth Certification in the Developing World', *World Politics*, 68(2), pp. 191–228.

Inter-American Court of Human Rights (2005) *Case of the Girls Yean and Bosico v. Dominican Republic*. Judgment of 8 September 2005 (Preliminary Objections, Merits, Reparations and Costs).

———— (2014) *Case of Expelled Dominicans and Haitians v. Dominican Republic*.

International Human Rights Clinic (2015) *Justice Derailed: The Uncertain Fate of Haitian Migrants and Dominicans of Haitian Descent in the Dominican Republic*. Baltimore, MD: Johns Hopkins School of Advanced International Studies.

ISI (2014) *The World's Stateless*. Tilburg: Institute on Statelessness and Inclusion.

———— (2020) *Locked In and Locked Out: The Impact of Digital Identity Systems on Rohingya Populations*. Tilburg: Institute on Statelessness and Inclusion.

James, C. L. R. (1938) *The Black Jacobins*. 2001st ed. London: Penguin.

Johnson, S. A. (2011) 'State-Led Growth and Development', in *Challenges in Health and Development*, pp. 71–101. Berlin: Springer Science+Business Media. Berlin.

Junta Central Electoral (JCE) (2014) *Invitamos a todas las personas contenidas en este listado a pasar por las Oficialías del Estado Civil que aparecen en esta relación a recoger su acta de registro de inscripción que le acredita como dominicanos en virtud de la Ley No. 169/14, Listin Diario.* Santo Domingo. Available at: http://www.listindiario.com/Themes/Default/Content/img/jce.pdf.

Ladner, D., Jensen, E. G., and Saunders, S. E. (2014) 'A Critical Assessment of Legal Identity: What It Promises and What It Delivers', *Hague Journal on the Rule of Law,* 6: 47–74.

Lawrance, B. N., and Stevens, J. (2017) *Citizenship in Question: Evidentiary Birthright and Statelessness.* Durham, NC: Duke University Press.

Listin Diario (2014) *Rosario dice nueva cédula incluirá escudo de la bandera y será expresión de la dominicanidad.* Available at: https://www.listindiario.com/la-republica/2014/02/06/309707/rosario-dice-nueva-cedula-incluira-escudo-de-la-bandera-y-sera-expresion-de-la-dominicanidad.

Lizardo, J. (2005) *El Gasto Social en la República Dominicana 1995–2005: Tendencias y Desafíos.* Santo Domingo: Unidad de Análisis Económico, Secretariado Técnico de la Presidencia

Lozano, Wilfredo (2008) *La paradoja de las migraciones: El Estado Dominicano frente a la inmigración Haitiana.* Editorial UNIBE, FLACSO, SJRM. Santo Domingo: Editor Búho.

Lyon, D. (2009) *Identifying Citizens: ID Cards as Surveillance.* Cambridge: Wiley.

Lyon, J. (2018) 'Inheriting Illegality: Race, Statelessness, and Dominico-Haitian Activism in the Dominican Republic', doctoral thesis, Florida International University.

Mahapatra, P., Shibuya, K., Lopez, A., Coullare, F., Chlapati Rao, C., and Szreter, S. (2007) 'Civil Registration Systems and Vital Statistics: Successes and Missed Opportunities', *Lancet,* 370(9599), pp. 1653–63.

Manby, B. (2018) '"Legal identity" and Biometric Identification in Africa', *Migration and Citizenship: Newsletter of the American Political Science Association's Organized Section on Migration and Citizenship,* 6(2), pp. 54–59.

———— (2020) '"Legal Identity for All" and Statelessness: Opportunity and Threat at the Junction of Public and Private International Law', *Statelessness and Citizenship Review,* 2(2), pp. 248–71.

Manly, M., and van Waas, L. (2014) Musa 'Tilburg Law Review' *Statelessness Special Issue, Journal of International and European Law,* 19(1–2): 11–19 Leiden: Martinus Nijhoff.

Márquez, G., Berkman, H., Pagés, C., Gandelman, N., Gandelman, E., Calónico, S., Azevedo, V., Payne, M., Cárdenas, J.C., Duryea, S., Chaparro, J.C., Lora,E., Ñopo, H. R., Mazza, J., Ripani, L., Chong, A. E., Polanía, S., Márquez, G., Bouillon, C.P., and León, G. (2007) *Outsiders? The Changing Patterns of Exclusion in Latin America and the Caribbean. 2008 Report.* Cambridge, MA: Harvard University Press.

Martí i Puig, S., Sánchez-Ancochea, D., and Stein, A. (2015) Sistematización de la implementación de Progresando con Solidaridad. Salamanca: Fundación General de la Universidad de Salamanca.

Martínez, S. (2014) 'The Price of Confrontation: International Retributive Justice and the Struggle for Haitian-Dominican Rights', in Andreopoulos, G., and Arat, Z. (eds) *The Uses and Misuses of Human Rights: A Critical Approach to Advocacy,* pp. 141–80. New York: Palgrave.

———— (2015) 'Samuel Martinez on "Anti-Haitian Exclusionism in the Dominican Republic"', YouTube video, Center for Religion, Ethics and Culture. Available at: https://www.youtube.com/watch?v=TLLUztLPJkk.

Martínez, S., and Wooding, B. (2017) 'El antihaitianismo en la República Dominicana:¿un giro biopolítico? *Migración y Desarrollo,* 15(28), pp. 95–123.

Mayes, A. J. (2014) *The Mulatto Republic: Class, Race, and Dominican National Identity.* Gainesville: University Press of Florida.

Mayes, A. J., and Jayaram, K. C. (eds) (2018) *Transnational Hispaniola: New Directions in Haitian and Dominican Studies*. Gainesville: University of Florida Press.

MEPyD (2012) *La Ley Orgánica de la Estrategia Nacional de Desarrollo de la República Dominicana 2030 (END)*. Santo Domingo: Gobierno de la República Dominicana.

Mercedes, R. (2018) *Denuncian intensiones en EEUU de fusionar RD con Haití, CDN Digital*. Available at: https://www.cdn.com.do/2018/08/14/denuncian-intensiones-eeuu-fusionar-rd-haiti/.

Mintz, S. W. (1966) 'The Caribbean as a Sociocultural Area', *Journal of World History*, 9(4), pp. 912–37.

Mintz, S. W., and Price, S. (eds) (1985) *Caribbean Contours*. Baltimore, MD: Johns Hopkins Studies in Atlantic History and Culture.

Mitchell, C. (2014) *Decentralization and Party Politics in the Dominican Republic*. Basingstoke, Hampshire: Palgrave Macmillan.

Moya Pons, F. (2009) *La Otra Historia Dominicana*. 2nd ed. Santo Domingo: Librería La Trinitaria.

Nussbaum, M., and Sen, A. (eds) (1993) *The Quality of Life*. Oxford: Clarendon Press.

OSJI (2018) 'A Community-Based Practitioner's Guide. Documenting Citizenship & Other Forms of Legal Identity', Report by the Open Society Justice Initiative, New York.

Parker, K. M. (2015) *Making Foreigners: Immigration and Citizenship Law in America, 1600–2000*. Cambridge: Cambridge University Press.

Paulino, E. (2015) *Dividing Hispaniola: The Dominican Republic's Border Campaign against Haiti, 1930–1961*. Pittsburgh, PA: University of Pittsburgh Press.

Peña Batlle, M. A. (1988) *Historia de la cuestión fronteriza dominico-haitiana*. Santo Domingo: Sociedad Dominicana de Bibliofilos.

Perez Hazel, Y. (2014) 'Sensing Difference: Whiteness, National Identity and Belonging in the Dominican Republic', *Transforming Anthropology, Journal of the Association of Black Anthropologists*, 22(2), pp. 78–91.

——— (2016) 'Whiteness in Paradise: Japanese Immigrant Narratives of Identity, Collective Action, and Japan's National Responsibility', *Asian Ethnicity*, 17(3), pp. 435–55.

Perrault, N., and Begoña, A. (2011) 'A Rights-Based Approach to Birth Registration in Latin America and the Caribbean', in *Challenges Newsletter. The Right to an Identity: Birth Registration in Latin America and the Caribbean*, pp. 4–12. Santiago de Chile: Economic Commission for Latin America and the Caribbean.

Petrozziello, A. J., Hintzen, A., and González Díaz, J. C. (2014) *Género y el riesgo de apatridia para la población de ascendencia haitiana en los bateyes de la República Dominicana*. Santo Domingo: Centro para la Observación Migratoria y el Desarrollo en el Caribe (OBMICA).

Pichardo Muñiz, A. (2012) 'Estudio Línea Base (ELB) y Evaluación del Impacto (EI) Proyecto de Inversión en la Protección Social (PIPS) de la República Dominicana: Informe Final Definitivo', Report by Gabinete de Coordinación de Políticas Públicas, Santo Domingo.

——— (2014) *Proyecto de Inversión en la Protección Social (PIPS) Estudio Línea Base y Evaluación del Impacto*. Santo Domingo: Gabinete de Coordinación de Políticas Públicas.

Presidencia de la República Dominicana (2013) *República Dominicana explica ante OEA estrategia regularización de extranjeros*. Available at: https://presidencia.gob.do/noticias/republica-dominicana-explica-ante-oea-estrategia-regularizacion-de-extranjeros.

Pribble, J. (2013) *Welfare and Party Politics in Latin America*. New York: Cambridge University Press.

Programa Solidaridad (2006) *Manual Operativo del Programa Solidaridad:*. Santo Domingo.

Regalia, F., and Robles, M. (2005) *Social Assistance, Poverty and Equity in the Dominican Republic, Economic and Sector Study Series*. Washington, DC: Gabinete de Política Social.

Riveros, N. (2014) 'El Estado de la cuestión de la población de los bateyes dominicanos en relación a la documentación', Report by Inter-American Development Bank, Santo Domingo.

Robert F. Kennedy Human Rights, American Jewish World Service, Centro de Desarrollo Sostenible, and United Nations Democracy Fund (2017) *Dreams Deferred: The Struggle of Dominicans of Haitian Descent to Get Their Nationality Back*. Washington, DC: Robert F. Kennedy Human Rights.

Roorda, E. P. (1998) *The Dictator Next Door: The Good Neighbor Policy and the Trujillo Regime in the Dominican Republic, 1930–1945*. Durham, NC: Duke University Press.

Saavedra, J. E., and Garcia, S. (2012) 'Impacts of Conditional Cash Transfer Programs on Educational Outcomes in Developing Countries: A Meta-Analysis', RAND Working Paper, pp. 1–63.

Sagás, E. (2002) *Race and Politics in the Dominican Republic*. Gainesville: University of Florida Press.

———— (2018) 'To Be, but Not to Be: (Re)defining Citizenship and Dominicanidad', LASA Paper, Department of Ethnic Studies, Colorado State University.

Sánchez, R. (2006) *Hacia un Plan Nacional de Documentación de Dominicanos(as): Diagnóstico, Objetivos, Lineamientos Estratégicos y Componentes*. Santo Domingo: Serie Protección Social.

San Miguel, P. L. (1997) *La isla imaginada: Historia, identidad y utopía en La Española*. Santo Domingo: Isla Negra.

———— (2005) *The Imagined Island: History, Identity & Utopia in Hispaniola*. Durham, NC: Consortium in Latin American Studies at the University of North Carolina at Chapel Hill and Duke University.

Scott, J. C. (1998) *Seeing Like a State: How Certain Schemes to Improve the Human Condition Have Failed*. New Haven: Yale University Press.

Sears, N. (2014) 'Repealing Birthright Citizenship: How the Dominican Republic's Recent Court Decision Reflects an International Trend', *Law and Business Review of the Americas*, 20, pp. 423–48.

Seltzer, W., and Anderson, M. (2001) 'The Dark Side of Numbers: The Role of Population Data Systems in Human Rights Abuses', *Social Research*, 68(2), pp. 481–513.

Sen, A. (1999) *Development as Freedom*. New York: Knopf.

Shipley, K. (2015) 'Stateless: Dominican-Born Grandchildren of Haitian Undocumented Immigrants in the Dominican Republic', *Transnational Law & Contemporary Problems*, 20(3): 459–87.

Simmons, K. E. (2009) *Reconstructing Racial Identity and the African Past in the Dominican Republic*. Gainesville: University Press of Florida.

van der Straaten, J. (2020) 'Identification for Development It Is Not. "Inclusive and Trusted Digital ID Can Unlock Opportunities for the Vulnerable" – A Review', Civil Registration Centre for Development (CRC4D), (November).

Suprema Corte de Justicia (2014) *Junta Central Electoral v. Ana María Belique Delba*. Resolución 1342–2014.

Thornton, B. J., and Ubiera, D. I. (2019) 'Caribbean Exceptions: The Problem of Race and Nation in Dominican Studies', *Latin American Research Review*, 54(2), pp. 413–28. doi:10.25222/larr.346.

Tonkiss, K. (2018) *The Windrush Scandal and the Incoherence of Liberal Exclusion, Discover Society.* Available at: https://discoversociety.org/2018/06/05/the-windrush-scandal-and-the-incoherence-of-liberal-exclusion/.

Tonkiss, K., and Bloom, T. (2015) 'Theorising Noncitizenship: Concepts, Debates and Challenges', *Citizenship Studies*, 19(8), pp. 837–52.

Toque Profundo (1993) 'Dios salve al viajero' (song). Santo Domingo.

Torpey, J. (2000) *The Invention of the Passport: Surveillance, Citizenship and the State.* Cambridge: Cambridge Studies in Law and Society, Cambridge University Press.

Torres-Saillant, S. (1998) 'The Tribulations of Blackness: Stages in Dominical Racial Identity', *Latin American Perspectives*, 25(3), pp. 126–46.

Tribunal Constitucional (2013) 'Sentencia TC/0168/13. Referencia: Expediente número TC-05-2012-0077'. Santo Domingo.

Trouillot, M.-R. (1991) 'From Planters' Journals to Academia: The Haitian Revolution as Unthinkable History', *Journal of Caribbean History*, 25(1–2), pp. 81–99.

Turits, R. L. (2002) *Foundations of Depotism: Peasants, the Trujillo Regime and Modernity in Dominican History.* Redwood City, CA: Stanford University Press.

UNDP (2010) *Política social II: capacidades y derechos. Análisis y propuestas de políticas sociales en República Dominicana.* Santo Domingo.

UNHCR (2003) *The 1954 Convention relating to the Status of Stateless Persons: Implementation within the European Union Member States and Recommendations for Harmonisation.* Geneva: UNCHR.

——— (2010) 'UNHCR Action to Address Statelessness: A Strategy Note', *International Journal of Refugee Law*, 22(2), pp. 297–335.

UNHCR and Plan International (2012) *Under the Radar and Under Protected: The Urgent Need to Address Stateless Children's Rights.* Woking: Plan International.

UNICEF (2007) *Progress for Children: A World Fit for Children-Statistical Review.* New York. Available at: http://www.unicef.org/publications/files/Progress_for_Children_No_6_revised.pdf.

——— (2013) *A Passport to Protection: A Guide to Birth Registration Programming.* New York: UNICEF.

United Nations (2015) *Transforming Our World: The 2030 Agenda for Sustainable Development.* New York. Available at: sustainabledevelopment.un.org.

US Government Cable (2005) *Dominicans Angered by Verdict at Inter-American Court of Human Rights.* Santo Domingo. Available at: http://wikileaks.org/plusd/cables/05SANTODOMINGO4611_a.html.

——— (2007) *Update on Maneuvers against Sonia Pierre, Haitian-Dominican Advocate.* Santo Domingo. Available at: https://wikileaks.org/plusd/cables/07SANTODOMINGO768_a.html.

——— (2008a) *Fernandez's Priority: A New Constitution.* Santo Domingo. Available at: https://wikileaks.org/plusd/cables/08SANTODOMINGO1608_a.html.

——— (2008b) *Open Society Justice Initiative Condemns DR Birth Registration System.* Santo Domingo. Available at: https://wikileaks.org/plusd/cables/08SANTODOMINGO192_a.html.

——— (2009a) *Dominicans Begin Work on Implementing Their 2004 Immigration Law.* Santo Domingo. Available at: http://wikileaks.org/plusd/cables/09SANTODOMINGO236_a.html.

——— (2009b) *Government Announces Documentation Initiative.* Santo Domingo. Available at: https://wikileaks.org/plusd/cables/09SANTODOMINGO706_a.html.

Vandenabeele, C. (2011) 'To Register or Not to Register? Legal Identity, Birth Registration, and Inclusive Development', in *Children without a State: A Global Human Rights Challenge*, pp. 307–30. Cambridge, MA: MIT Press.

Varela, J. R. (2015) 'Trump's Immigration Plan Would Require Every Latino to Show Their Papers, Please', *Guardian*. Available at: https://www.theguardian.com/commentisfree/2015/aug/31/donald-trump-immigration-plan-would-require-every-latino-to-show-papers.

van Waas, L. (2015) *The Right to a Legal Identity or the Right to a Legal ID?, European Network on Statelessness*. Available at: https://www.statelessness.eu/blog/right-legal-identity-or-right-legal-id.

Wade, P. (1993) *Blackness and Race Mixture: The Dynamics of Racial Identity in Colombia*. Baltimore, MD: Johns Hopkins University Press.

———— (2005) 'Rethinking Mestizaje: Ideology and Lived Experience', *Journal of Latin American Studies*, 37(2), pp. 239–57.

Weitzberg, K. (2017) *We Do Not Have Borders: Greater Somalia and the Predicaments of Belonging in Kenya*. Ohio: Ohio University Press.

Weitzberg, K., Cheesman, M., and Martin, A. (2021) 'Between Surveillance and Recognition: Rethinking Digital Identity in Aid', *Big Data and Society*, 8(1): 1–7. doi:10.1177/20539517211006744.

Wheeler, E. M. (2015) 'Race, Legacy, and Lineage in the Dominican Republic Shifting Paradigms', *Black Scholar*, 45(2), pp. 34–44.

World Bank (2004a) *Social Crisis Response Adjustment Loan (SCRAL) between Dominican Republic and International Bank for Reconstruction and Development, No.7215-DO*. Santo Domingo: World Bank.

———— (2004b) *World Development Report 2004: Making Services Work for Poor People, Banque mondiale*. Washington, DC: World Bank.

———— (2007) *Project Appraisal Document on a Proposed Loan in the Amount of US$19.4 Million to the Dominican Republic for a Social Protection Investment Project. Dominican Republic Social Protection Investment Loan. Report No: 36299-DO*. Washington, DC: World Bank.

———— (2013) *Inclusion Matters: The Foundation for Shared Prosperity*. Washington, DC: International Bank for Reconstruction and Development/World Bank.

Zolberg, A. R. (2006) *Nation by Design: Immigration Policy in the Fashioning of America*. New York: Russell Sage Foundation with Harvard University Press.

STAKEHOLDER INTERVIEWS

1. Mia Harbitz, former Inter-American Development Bank lead specialist in registration and identity management (1998–2015) (16 and 19 July 2019 via Skype)[1]
2. Samuel Carlson, principal economist and social inclusion, education and childhood development specialist responsible for the elaboration and implementation of the World Bank Social Protection Investment Project 2004–7 (6 September 2016 via Skype)
3. Miriam Rodríguez de Simó, former director of the Unique System for Beneficiaries (SIUBEN) (10 August 2016 at the Ministry of Economy, Planning and Development (MEPyD), Santo Domingo)
4. Van Elder Espinal Martínez, former director of the Social Subsidies Administration (ADESS) (11 August 2016 in a coffee shop, Piantini, Santo Domingo)
5. Fernando Reyes Castro, former director of Programa Solidaridad (17 August 2016 at the office of former vice president Rafael Francisco Alburquerque de Castro, Santo Domingo)
6. Enrique Ogando, former director of the Legal Identity Documentation Component, Social Protection Investment Project (CDD-PIPS) (23 August 2016 at the offices of the Executive Commission for Health Sector Reform, CERSS, in Gazcue, Santo Domingo)
7. Brígida Sabino, civil registry official, former director of Late Birth Registrations and current director of the Inspections Department at the Central Electoral Board (JCE) (25 August 2016 at the JCE Inspections Department in Santo Domingo)

1. The bulk of these interviews in this book were originally carried out as part of my doctoral thesis: Hayes de Kalaf, E. (2018) 'Making Foreign: Legal Identity, Social Policy and the Contours of Belonging in the Contemporary Dominican Republic', British Library EThOS.

8. Odalys Otero Núñez, director of the National School of Electoral Training and Civil Status (EFEC) (26 August 2016 at EFEC in La Castellana, Santo Domingo)

9. Arsénito Santana, a health worker at the Centre for Sustainable Development (Centro de Desarrollo Sostenible, CEDESO), a Dominican NGO (7 April 2016 at CEDESO head office in Tamayo, Bahoruco)

10. Yoni Tusen, community project development worker at 180° para la Cooperación y el Desarrollo, a Dominican NGO based in La Romana, (6 May 2016 in Guaymate, La Romana)

11. Midouard Confident, coordinator of *batey* outreach at 180° para la Cooperación y el Desarrollo, Dominican NGO based in La Romana, (6 May 2016 in Guaymate, La Romana)

12. Ana María Belique Delba, founder of Reconoci.do and employee at Centro Bonó, Dominican NGO; Ana was in a long-running dispute with the Dominican authorities over access to her Dominican national identity card (20 May 2016 at Centro Bonó, Mejoramiento Social, Santo Domingo)

13. Dr Bridget Wooding, director of the NGO Caribbean Migrants Observatory (OBMICA), Dominican NGO; OBMICA works with Haitian migrants and their descendants; it also facilitates dialogue between many international organisations and development agencies working on the Dominican case (19 August 2016 at the OBMICA office in Gazcue, Santo Domingo)

14. Lawyer Jenny Morón, who works with Haitian-descended populations affected by ruling 168-13, at the Movement of Haitian-Dominican Women (El Movimiento de Mujeres Dominico-Haitianas, MUDHA) (25 April 2016 at the MUDHA office in La Balsa de San Luis, East Santo Domingo)

15. María Martínez, caseworker at the Socio-Cultural Movement for Haitian Workers (Movimiento Socio Cultural para los Trabajadores Haitianos, MOSCTHA) (13 April 2016 at the MOSCTHA office in Villa Mella, Santo Domingo)

16. Juan Bolívar Díaz, Dominican journalist for *Hoy* newspaper and television presenter; Juan has been a prominent critic of recent registration measures (27 August 2016 at newspaper offices Periódico Hoy, Santo Domingo)

17. School director (Anon.) (4 May 2016 at a school in Guaymate, La Romana)

18. Dr Miguel Ceara Hatton, the economist, former director of the Office of Human Development at the United Nations Development Program (UNDP) and editor of the UNDP Social Policy publications (17 May 2016 at his home in Santo Domingo)

19. Leopoldo Artiles Gil, a sectorial specialist at the Dominican government (10 August 2016 at MEPyD, Santo Domingo)
20. Dr Antonio Morillo, the economist responsible for the development of all Dominican Poverty Maps since the 1990s (10 August 2016 at MEPyD, Santo Domingo)

INDEX

Milton Keynes UK
Ingram Content Group UK Ltd.
UKHW011415290823
427684UK00017B/351